THE TRUTH OF ECONOMY

ALSO BY FAISAL MALICK

10 Amazing Muslims Touched by God
The Political Spirit
Positioned to Bless
Here Comes Ishmael
The Destiny of Islam in the Endtimes

THE TRUTH OF ECONOMY

TURNING DOWNTURNS INTO UPTURNS

FAISAL MALICK

Copyright © 2017 by Faisal Malick

All rights reserved. No part of this publication may be reproduced, distributed, or transmitted in any form or by any means, including photocopying, recording, or other electronic or mechanical methods, without the prior written permission of the publisher, except in the case of brief quotations embodied in critical reviews and certain other noncommercial uses permitted by copyright law. For permission requests, write to the publisher, addressed "Attention: Permissions Coordinator," at the address below.

Plumbline Publishing
P.O. Box 31077
Langley, BC
V1M 0A9
www.PlumblinePublishing.com

- Scripture quotations marked (NIV) are taken from the Holy Bible, New International Version®, NIV®. Copyright © 1973, 1978, 1984, 2011 by Biblica, Inc.™ Used by permission of Zondervan. All rights reserved worldwide. www.zondervan.com The "NIV" and "New International Version" are trademarks registered in the United States Patent and Trademark Office by Biblica, Inc.™

- Scripture taken from the New King James Version®. Copyright © 1982 by Thomas Nelson. Used by permission. All rights reserved.

- Scripture quotations taken from the New American Standard Bible® (NASB), Copyright © 1960, 1962, 1963, 1968, 1971, 1972, 1973, 1975, 1977, 1995 by The Lockman Foundation

- Used by permission. www.Lockman.org

- Scripture quotations taken from the Amplified® Bible (AMP), Copyright © 2015 by The Lockman Foundation. Used by permission. www.Lockman.org

- Scripture quotations are taken from the Holy Bible, New Living Translation, copyright ©1996, 2004, 2007, 2013, 2015 by Tyndale House Foundation. Used by permission of Tyndale House Publishers, Inc., Carol Stream, Illinois 60188. All rights reserved.

- Scripture quotations marked MSG are taken from THE MESSAGE, copyright © 1993, 1994, 1995, 1996, 2000, 2001, 2002 by Eugene H. Peterson. Used by permission of NavPress. All rights reserved. Represented by Tyndale House Publishers, Inc.

Printed in Mexico
Cover and interior design by: Joseph Myers

ISBN 978-0-9993309-1-3

First Edition

THIS BOOK IS **DEDICATED** TO:

*Those who seek to make friends with money and align with its eternal
purpose—no matter how little or how much they have.
May you find a peaceful grace inherent in God's economy.
(Luke 16:9)*

Contents

Preface	vii
1: **The m word:** making peace with money	1
2: **Changing our minds:** money in its proper place	29
3: **Safe:** the fear factor	53
4: **The gods of economy:** god or mammon	71
5: **All shaken up:** turning downturns into upturns	103
6: **Taking it to the bank:** wise investing	129
7: **The solomon effect:** royal generosity	149
8: **Weather forecast:** upturns, downturns, and a pizza	177

LET ME **PREFACE** BY SAYING:

At times, it seems there's one big elephant-in-the-room that controls our lives: Money. Marriages fall apart because of it. World leaders have influence when they have it and if it's status you want, it can be purchased. Money talks...loudly!

We've developed thoughts, ideas, and concepts about money. Even if you've never thought much about wealth and money, all of us are flooded by messages from culture, marketing gurus, family, educational systems, and religion. Each one vies for our attention so they can share their own perspective about money's purpose and use.

By now your stress level may have begun to rise and you're wondering if one more book or one more insight can bring hope. You're probably leafing through these pages anticipating the same old answers. But you'd be mistaken.

While most books about money build a foundation firmly on management and "working harder" strategies, *The Truth of Economy* builds on a foundation on purpose. What is the primary purpose of money in your life? The answer might seem obvious: to increase my buying power. However, simply shifting the purpose of money in your life creates a powerful conduit for wealth creation. It might shock you to know that the Creator of the universe has a purpose for money and He'll give you the power to create wealth. He has designed the system and principles necessary to reap from a purpose-driven investment and provide all you need without paycheck-to-paycheck worry.

"And you shall remember the Lord your God, for it is He who gives you power to get wealth, that He may establish His covenant which He swore to your fathers, as it is this day." (Deuteronomy 8:18, NKJV)

Within these pages, you will discover a new way to see, think, and behave. Yes, this book is about money, wealth, and understanding economic structures but its primary focus is "looking behind the curtain" and clearly seeing money's eternal purpose.

No matter your upbringing or economic position, you need an open mind as the concepts within stretch you and call into question some of your tightly held beliefs about money and wealth.

We will learn from some of the wealthiest people in history and dive into the two economic systems that control the flow of money. We will discuss pitfalls that come with trying to build wealth on the wrong purpose and provide principles to make the necessary changes to establish generational wealth. Your fears will be met with hopeful solutions.

I'm honored to journey through this book with you.

Faisal Malick

CHAPTER 1

THE M WORD:
MAKING PEACE WITH MONEY

*"I would give all the wealth of the world,
and all the deeds of all the heroes, for one true vision."*
Henry David Thoreau

If Henry David Thoreau walked from his rustic cabin into the modern-day business world, he would find his words to be prescient ones. Vision is priceless. And though he would undoubtedly loathe to set his Walden-esque eyes upon an electric blue IKEA building large enough to house a small country, he would likely admire the humility of the company's beginnings and the simplicity of the vision statement it represents.

IKEA's roots are in a small village in the south of Sweden. The Company began simply, selling pens and pencils, and within 10 years grew to a flagship retail store that would go on to change an entire furniture distribution industry. IKEA figured out that the way to sell inexpensive yet attractive furniture was by sending most items out the door flat-packaged and ready for the customer to assemble at home. This concept drove cost way down for consumers and volume way up for factories[1].

Early on, IKEA seemed to figure out a few things about people. First, one of the primary things we learn and recognize are shapes. So when they set out to write a vision statement they didn't bury it in too much text. Under the aptly titled page, "The IKEA Vision," they drew a blue triangle.

---

1 About Us. (2012-2016). Milestones In Our History – Inter IKEA Group. Inter IKEA Systems B.V. Retrieved from: http://inter.ikea.com/en/about-us/milestones/

And at the top of the triangle they stated their vision simply:

To create a better everyday life for the many people.

The second corner of the triangle explains the business idea—in other words, how they plan to fulfill the vision. In IKEA's case this is:

We shall offer a wide range of well-designed, functional home furnishing products at prices so low that as many people as possible will be able to afford them.

The third corner of the triangle talks about how the company is going to use people – future employees—to fulfill the vision.

Why was IKEA so successful and why does it continue to be so? They make an attractive product. They make it readily available in large warehouse stores and through thriving catalog and web sales. They install play lands for kids and offer a pleasant, well-lit shopping experience and a cafeteria with enough food options to keep the entire family fed and happy for as long as they can stay (which is sometimes for several hours).

IKEA is also so straightforward about vision that you can't miss it. IKEA seems to say: we will do everything mentioned above. And on top of that we will make everything, even the meatballs you eat for lunch, so cheap that if you can read the price tag you can likely afford it[2].

They don't shy away from a straightforward acknowledgment of our personal finances, a bold tactic given how reluctant we are to talk about money.

And we really don't like to talk about money.

We don't want to talk about having too much of it and we definitely don't want to talk about having too little of it. We revere it. We

---

2   The IKEA Vision. (1999-2016). Inter IKEA Sytems B.V. The IKEA Vision. Retrieved from: http://www.ikea.com/ms/en_CA/the_ikea_story/working_at_ikea/our_vision.html

fear it. We love it and we hate it. Sometimes we're convinced that God wants us to be poor. We're pretty sure He doesn't want us to be rich. There are temptations everywhere we turn.

We are reluctant to talk about money because our toil and struggle with it are constant. Sometimes hoping for it seems in vain, though the pursuit of it for some can be addictively thrilling. Whether it is blessing or curse, capitalism or socialism, rich or poor, anxious days and sleepless nights or "it doesn't really count because we're on vacation," one thing nearly all of us have in common is this:

It's time to make peace with money.]

To do that we need to be clear about the vision for our money. Money affects every day of our lives and we exchange it constantly for everything we need and want. Without vision we are in a constant state of being in the moment. We have no direction or hope or enthusiasm. We leave ourselves vulnerable to fear.

We need some clarity. We need vision.

It's time to make peace with money.

VISION

So what is vision?

Vision is what you are working toward.

It is a mental image of how you picture your future. It provides guidance for what we want to achieve in the short, middle and long term. It functions as the North Star. It's a sort of plumbline for the future, helping us to direct what our life, down to even the most humble task, is meant to accomplish every day.

A good vision, whether it is for a company, family, or other group, is written or spoken so concisely that future employees, generations of team members, can repeat it easily. Vision encourages people to focus on what's important and how to align their resources toward it.

Examples of Good Vision

Good vision statements embed themselves into a culture through a unified sense of purpose, improving decision-making with clarity about the big picture. They highlight priorities and are succinct yet powerful. They influence billions of people to exchange billions of dollars using few words:

"A world without Alzheimer's disease"

Alzheimer's Association[3]

"To be the company that best understands and satisfies the product, service and self-fulfillment needs of women, globally"

Avon[4]

"We will lead the fight against extinction"

San Diego Zoo[5]

"Be the safest, most customer-focused and successful transportation company in the world"

Norfolk Southern[6]

---

3 Alzheimer's Association. (2017). Retrieved from http://alz.org
4 Avon Products, Inc. (2016). About Us. Retrieved from http://www.avoncompany.com/aboutavon
5 San Diego Zoo Global. (2017). San Diego Zoo Global Mission and Vision. San Retrieved from http://zoo.sandiegozoo.org/content/san-diego-zoo-global-mission-and-vision
6 Norfolk Southern Corp. (2017). The NS Story Vision & Values. Retrieved from www.

> "To be the best food company, growing a better world"
>
> Kraft Heinz[7]

And "good business leaders," says Jack Welch, former Chairman of General Electric, "create a vision, articulate the vision, passionately own the vision, and relentlessly drive it to completion.[8]"

It is challenging to speak to what others see and feel to motivate and draw them in. A vision must inspire and enlist others with exciting future possibilities without becoming shortsighted in the process.

Vision Fixation

A good, clear vision is great, but leaders who fall in love with their own strategies and are committed to preserving them at all cost – regardless of the changes in market realities – are doomed to eventually fail.

We have a tendency to get comfortable with success. We think that won't affect us and old systems will work inside of new ones. We are prone to the myopia that if we just continue to focus on what made us successful in the first place, we will continue to be successful into the future.

Even passionate visionaries with nearly perfect vision statements are at risk because they are just that: nearly perfect. So, we need a perfect vision. One that points to a purpose, aligns our talents and our resources, and brings us into our future. It needs to be

---

nscorp.com/content/nscorp/en/the-norfolk-wouthern-story/vision-and-values.
7 The Kraft Heinz Company. (2017). Vision & Values – Kraft Heinz Careers. Retrieved from: http://kraftheinz.site.staffcv.com/vision-values/
8 Tichy, N and Charan, R. (September-October 1989). Speed, Simplicity, Self-confidence: An Interview with Jack Welch. Harvard Business Review. Retrieved from https://hbr.org/1989/09/speed-simplicity-self-confidence-an-interview-with-jack-welch

able to withstand fluctuating markets, short-sighted decision making, and social progress. In other words: it needs to be a perfect vision for an imperfect world.

We have just the thing.

God's Vision

Solomon, arguably the wealthiest man to ever live, said, "without a vision the people perish."[9]

Solomon in his writings takes the definition of the word vision even further. In the Hebrew language, vision means "a revelation of God's heart for mankind." It means to see into the heart of God and capture His intent for all people. Any vision directly or indirectly inspired by God always brings hope and benefits our world.

Vision can cause economies of nations to thrive and its citizens to prosper. Without vision businesses fail, families fall apart, and cities cannot flourish. Vision laser focuses on where we are headed and forms all our decisions, great and small.

The source of vision is as important as the vision. Hitler's vision led to the death of millions of people and the Holocaust. Obviously this was not the kind of vision Solomon was referring to. We could say the same of the horrific vision of ISIS and other terrorist groups. Often the people perish simply because in the absence of Gods vision for mankind demonic vision prevails. We should never permit the torch of God's vision to be extinguished.

God's economy is directed by His vision. Money has a specific purpose in the scope of God's vision. God's economy supersedes the world's economy but works within an earthly economy with a two-fold plan: First, He is diligent to fulfill His Covenant, a promised estate, to mankind (more on this later). And second,

---

9 Proverbs 29:18

God's vision is able to flex and breathe to accommodate changes. He even uses downturns in the economy to accomplish this. His economy not only operates within the ups and downs of the regular, earthly economy, it actually thrives during the downturns.

God the master visionary tells us exactly what His vision promises. Let me share with you His vision progressively revealed through the ages.

God's vision is to establish and confirm the Abrahamic Covenant, and to fulfill this by blessing all people of the world through the gospel of the Kingdom in the person of Jesus Christ.[10]

God is the ultimate visionary. He saw everything when there was nothing. He knew you before you were born. And God made a promise to bless you and all mankind (that's us!). Mankind, then, must understand and participate in this promise to flourish.

However, let's be clear. We aren't responsible for looking high and low, hoping to one day find a vision. Our job is to make room for God's vision. His vision is the key to sustainability. It's recession-proof. Your participation in God's vision not only changes your view of money; it changes the focus of your entire life. Make room for God's vision in your life and He'll make room for you in His vision. In doing so you will discover your assignment which is your role in His vision. This is God's plan, for you, for the Church in general, and for all the people of the world.

We are going to discuss what this contractual promise, this Covenant, is, what it means to us, and how money is connected to it. We are going to address some of our fears about money, our history of financial slavery, how God used and continues to use economic downturns to prosper His followers, and how God's vision and the wisdom that comes along with it changes everything. Literally. It changes everything.

---

10 Genesis 12:3, Matthew 28:18-20, Galatians 3:8, 17,

God did a lot of talking to people in dreams. And when God appeared to Abraham in a vision – in a waking dream – He indeed had something very life changing to say. He shared His vision with Abraham and made him a promise, a Covenant. And this Covenant would change a nation, would change the world, and it can still change our hearts today.

THE ABRAHAMIC COVENANT

Before we get into the Abrahamic Covenant, let's gain some understanding about covenants in general. We are probably all familiar with the idea of covenants because we all make them, at least informally, all the time.

A covenant is a contractual agreement between two parties, two people, or two organizations. It can be formal, like a promise from a bank to a homeowner that they will provide a mortgage at certain terms in exchange for the homeowner's agreement that they will pay back the mortgage in the amount and on the schedule that the bank contract stipulates. A covenant can also be informal, like the trust between two friends or the symbiotic relationship between two animals, as in: I will eat the bugs off your back if you agree to not to make me your dinner.

There are two types of covenants: conditional and unconditional.

A conditional or bilateral agreement is the one we are most familiar with. It means that both parties agree to fulfill specific conditions in order for the covenant to remain valid. If either party doesn't fulfill their end of the agreement, the covenant is no longer any good. The house goes back to the bank. The crocodile eats the bird.

In an unconditional or unilateral covenant both parties forge an agreement, but only one party must act in order to fulfill it. Nothing is required of the other party.

In either case, a covenant involves the exchange of property or actions to seal the covenant. To honor this in ancient times, the severing of an animal or animals often sealed covenants, and the two people or parties would pass between the severed pieces as a sign of their agreement. This was serious business. It implied that if you broke the covenant you would be met with a similar fate. It meant you were willing to fulfill the covenant with the cost of your life.

It was into this era of severed animals and bloody agreements that God appeared to an elderly Hebrew man with a promise in the form of a covenant that is still valid today. The Jewish nation was about to be born. And a guy named Abraham was going to make it happen.

God's Covenant With Abraham[11]

God came to Abraham in a vision.[12]

"Leave your native country, your relatives, and your father's family and go to the land that I will show you. I will make you into a great nation. I will bless you and make you famous, and you will be a blessing to others. I will bless those who bless you and curse those who treat you with contempt. All the families on earth will be blessed through you." (Gen 12:1-3, NLT)

Remember how we mentioned that God had a habit of speaking to people in dreams? God came to Abraham in a vision and promised him land, protection, fame, and blessing. He promised Abraham, who at the time had no children of his own, as many descendants as there were stars in the sky. And most importantly, God shared His vision with Abraham to bless all mankind through his seed and promised redemption—God's forgiveness of sins into the future.

In the book of Galatians, a letter to a New Testament church, faith in Jesus Christ is explained as a confirmation of this Covenant.

---

11 Genesis 15:19
12 Acts 7:2

And the Scripture, foreseeing that God would justify the Gentiles by faith, preached the gospel to Abraham beforehand, saying, "In you all the nations shall be blessed."

And this I say, that the law, which was four hundred and thirty years later, cannot annul the covenant that was confirmed before by God in Christ,[a] that it should make the promise of no effect. (Galatians 3:8, 17, NKJV)

So you can see the Covenant God made with Abraham is still valid today in Christ.

God Binds Himself to The Covenant

First, God's Covenant with Abraham was unilateral, a willed estate promised to us and extends beyond the Jewish nation to the entire world. It required nothing of Abraham. Typical unconditional tradition involved a situation where the inferior party delivered animals while the superior swore the oath. The Abrahamic Covenant is part of a tradition of covenants like this that necessitated a sacrifice and symbolic act.

The Lord told him, "Bring me a three-year-old heifer, a three-year-old female goat, a three-year-old ram, a turtledove, and a young pigeon." So Abram presented all these to him and killed them. Then he cut each animal down the middle and laid the halves side by side; he did not, however, cut the birds in half. (Genesis 15:9-10, NLT)

Notice how the Lord asked Abraham to cut three animals in half and place them opposite each other as part of the ceremony to seal this Covenant. God categorizes all of humanity into three groups: Jews, Gentiles (all peoples including Muslims), and the Church made of Jew and Gentile alike who put their faith in Jesus Christ. God loves them all equally.

The heifer represented the Jewish people, the female goat represented the Gentile people and the ram represented the Church. This third category symbolized by the ram also represented the **ONE NEW MAN** referenced in the New Testament letter written to the church in Ephesus describing a new breed of humanity made of both Jew and Gentile in Christ.[13]

God then alone passed between the animals, in the form of a smoking fire pot and flaming torch signifying that He would be the One to fulfill this Covenant not only to Abraham and his descendants but also to the whole world.[14] I believe this was the pre-incarnate Christ who was to come as the ultimate sacrifice to fulfill the Abrahamic Covenant. The two birds that were not cut in half represented the Holy Spirit working in both old and new Covenants.

The scope of God's vision shared with Abraham in Genesis 12:2-3 would eventually encompass all of humanity, and the implications of this Covenant would be far-reaching. This vision becomes clearer as we embark on our journey through history and the biblical narrative of the interconnected stories of people's lives.

So what specifically did this promise entail? God made a promise in multiple parts, some of which were specific to land and his descendants and others that were to all of humanity and the future spiritual children of Abraham who would place their faith in his promised seed.

Note that God tells Abraham,

"Go from your country."

He asks Abram to go to the land He will show him.

"I will make you into a great nation. I will bless you and make you famous, and you will be a blessing to others. 3 I will bless those who bless you and curse those who treat you with contempt. All the families on earth will be blessed through

---
13 Ephesians 2:15, 2 Corinthians 5:17
14 Genesis 15:17-19

you." (Gen 12:2-3, NLT)

God Promises the Land

In addition to being unconditional, God's Covenant was also literal. God was going to give them land. Not heaven or relational currency or any other metaphorical use of the word. He was promising them property, as in the kind on which you can build a house, a city, or a parking lot. It's somewhere that Abraham's grandkids could ride their real bikes and skin their real knees.

He even specifies GPS coordinates: from the border of Egypt to the Euphrates River would be the land for Abraham and all his descendants. It's a real place and one that we could find on a map and go visit today.[15]

God gave the land to Abraham and centuries later his descendants would take control of it.

The only problem was this: at the time of Abraham's vision the land was occupied by a bunch of other people. So, the second part of the covenant came in the form of descendants. Lots of them.

God Promises Descendants

Abraham was 100 years old and 25 years into his relationship with God since God's first appearance when He shared His vision. He finally visited Abraham and his wife Sarah to fulfill the promise they would have a son.[16] Sarah was really old, too. Yet despite all biological reasons for this to seem impossible, Sarah became pregnant with a son, Isaac.

Isaac had two sons named Jacob and Esau. Jacob, whose name would later be changed to Israel by God (did you ever wonder where that name came from? Now you know!) was dad to 12

---
15 Gen 15:18-21
16 Hebrews 11:11

sons. Those 12 sons would become the 12 tribes of Israel, the ones who eventually settled in the land and multiplied. One of the 12 – Judah – would be the ancestor of a future King David and later another King named Jesus.[17]

And all those other people who were squatting in the land that God had promised to Abraham in his night vision? They had to go live somewhere else. (Mind you, some of them were killed in military campaigns during the conquest of this land.)[18]

In fact, God sweetened the deal in a way that was both hopeful and prophetic. Abraham was promised not only that he would have descendants, but that some of them would be future royalty:

"I will make you extremely fruitful. Your descendants will become many nations, and kings will be among them!" (Genesis 17:6, NLT)

Later, this royal promise to Abraham would be expanded though the promise made to his progeny, King David, often referred to as the Davidic Covenant. In the Davidic Covenant God promised this idea of perpetual kingship, rooted in the house of David. Jesus, the Messiah, would come from the line of David. God's rule over the whole world would be from David's line and this would transform history for all of mankind.[19] That includes us. This is our story, too!

"So all who put their faith in Christ (Jesus) share the same blessing Abraham received because of his faith." (Galatians 3:9, NLT)

God promised to provide descendants to carry on His Covenant. Not only that, He promised kings and nations, including a future Messiah, to descend from them. Not bad for a couple of retired people!

---

17 Matthew 1:3-17
18 Joshua 3:10
19 2 Samuel 7:12-16

Now the promised people were living in the land and God didn't want them to forget His promises. He asked Abraham to require a physical sign of the Covenant that would serve as a forever reminder.

And it was a little, let's say, unconventional.

God Gives a Sign of the Covenant Seed

God wanted to give a sign to Abraham's descendants; a physical reminder of His Covenant with them.[20] So, as God is known to do, He chose a solution so out of the box that no one else could take credit for it:

Circumcision.

Yes. This is weird, but it wasn't an idea plucked from thin air. It was an intimate mark on the flesh indicating the alignment of the people with God's blessing. It was something they couldn't undo. It was permanent.

It was a physical sign of the Covenant to remind them of the seed that was still to come – Jesus – who would fulfill God's vision for all mankind.

God Promises Blessing and Redemption

Remember how we said that a good vision is one that brings hope with it?

God's vision included blessing for Abraham, his descendants, and for all mankind through the promised Seed of the Messiah.[21]

"Through Christ Jesus, God has blessed the Gentiles with the same blessing he promised to Abraham, so that we who are believers might receive the promised Holy Spirit through faith." (Galatians 3:13-14, NLT)

---

20 Genesis 17:9-14
21 Galatians 3:16

This blessing is not only generational but also supernatural, and it works practically in your everyday life in the real world. Just look at the Jewish people and their history. Despite a long history of slavery, homelessness and economic downturns, the Jewish people continue to be proof of the blessing of the Abrahamic Covenant.

Today, Jewish people make up two percent of the American population but constitute 40% of American billionaires. One third of the people on the famous Forbes 400 list are of Jewish descent.[22] They are more heavily represented in scientific fields and have received more awards such as the Nobel Prize than any other group.[23] They possess higher IQs, on average 10 points higher, and have more super intelligent folks with IQs above 150 than any other population.[24] In other words, the Jewish people have not just survived oppression, famine, and genocide; they continue to flourish just as God promised.

We might be thinking, "What about the Mosaic Law or its relevance to all this?" The conditional Mosaic Covenant that was later made at Mt. Sinai brought the law, but didn't cancel the promise that God made to Abraham or to us:[25]

"And this I say, that the law, which was four hundred and thirty years later, cannot annul the covenant that was confirmed before by God in Christ, that it should make the promise of no effect." (Galatians 3:17, NKJV)

We have absolutely nothing to do with the obsolete Mosaic Covenant and its laws. Our blessing is connected to the Abrahamic Covenant and the principles of faith and inheritance that govern it.

---

22 Nolan, H. (2010). The Forbes 400: A Demographic Breakdown. Originally published at Gawker, Inc. Retrieved from http://www.businessinsider.com/the-forbes-400-a-demographic-breakdown-2010-9
23 Murray, C. (2007). Jewish Genius. Commentary Magazine. Retrieved from https://www.commentarymagazine.com/articles/jewish-genius/
24 Lynn, R. (2004). The Intelligence of American Jews. University of Ultser, Northern Ireland. Elsevier Ltd. Retrieved from http://www-personal.umich.edu/~negisama/asdf2.pdf
25 Exodus 19-24

The blessing of the Abrahamic Covenant is a willed estate that has been promised to us in Christ. The new Covenant is not just the intent (will) of God promised to us but also His last will and testament left to us though the blood of Jesus Christ. And just like someone has to die for the estate to be passed on, and just like a seed has to die in order for a flower to bloom, a death was required for us to become heirs of the promise and salvation.

God's vision is good. It brings His heart to ours.

The last will and testament of Jesus Christ is confirmation of the 4000-year-old Abrahamic Covenant that now makes the gospel first preached to Abraham available to everyone.[26] The Great Commission Jesus gave in Matthew 28 is an expression of this same gospel and God's vision to continue confirming the Abrahamic Covenant and blessing all families of the earth in Christ.[27]

This means you are one of the beneficiaries of the blessing of this Covenant and the redemption that accompanies it. You are one of the people God included in His vision.

Vision isn't a man-made idea. It isn't just about having a dream or having goals. Even though you may have those things, what is important is the message that comes with them and how the message is delivered. Dreams are the language of God and one way that He communicates with us. Vision isn't just to fulfill His purpose, it's also the vehicle He sometimes uses to communicate it.

And just like God came to Abraham with a vision for land, descendants and redemption, God has a dream about us, too.

---

26 Galatians 3:8
27 Matthew 24:14, Matthew 28:18-20

FITTING INTO THIS VISION

The Book of Us

Without a doubt, God has been busy. He had a big job talking to old guys in dreams, envisioning a promised land and then planning to fill it with His people. But believe it or not, while He was busy doing this he was already thinking about you and me.

"You saw me before I was born. Every day of my life was recorded in your book. Every moment was laid out before a single day had passed." (Psalm 139:16, NLT)

When you weren't even yet created God saw you and fashioned the days of your life before you were born. He knew the number of hairs on your head and the number of your days. He knew where you would be born and live. He's planned a life for you. He is premeditated in His purpose.

Now that's vision.

What's more, He's not controlling your life to bring about that vision. He's left you free to make decisions – free to ride the ebb and flow of the fluctuation of free will—but He has written His dream about you just the same. It's why you are the way you are. It's what makes you, you. He wrote a bestseller about you and put it in His heavenly library, and if you could open the pages of that book you would begin to understand God's heart for you, His love for you, and His grace for you—how He sees you.

God's vision dates back before time and every story, even your story, is a continual revelation of this. He is such a visionary that before the world existed, God knew Jesus would die for the sins of mankind. He planned this ahead of time so we could come into a covenant, an intimate relationship with Him that no one and no evil could separate us.

God already had Abraham in mind when he came up with that plan. God says he already had you in mind, too.[28]

God's vision is good. It brings His heart to ours. It comes equipped with inspiration, vitality, and vigor. The Abrahamic Covenant is rich with potential to redeem all mankind. It is eternal and will find further expression in the return of Jesus the Messiah and throughout eternity as we who are of faith inherit the cosmos. God's vision for mankind, and for each of us individually, is potent and clear.

Our job is simply to align with it.

Aligning With God's Vision

Before man was created and sinned against God, God had already made provision to redeem and buy him back.[29] God already made room for grace.

And here's how He did it: He gave us autonomy over our choices. We've been asked to align with good or to align with evil. He respects us and has given us governance over the earth. The world is full of chaos and evil because we are free to choose and the responsibility to do something about it is also in our stewardship.

How does a good God full of love allow evil to happen? It's a good question and you are not alone in asking it. In fact, people have been asking this for as long as we've had recorded history. The answer is: God gave us free will to choose good or evil and in doing so, He gave us His vision – something to work toward and to focus on – in the form of His Covenant.

Habakkuk asked the same thing. Habakkuk was an Old Testament prophet and he wrote succinctly about his frustration with this issue. "My nation is a mess," he told God, "it's full of

---
28 Psalm 139:16
29 Revelation 13:8

corruption. Where are you in the midst of this turmoil? How could your pure eyes see evil?" the prophet cried out to God.[30]

God's answer is: I am working behind the scenes and I have a plan. Be patient.

Write my answer plainly on tablets, so that a runner can carry the correct message to others. This vision is for a future time. It describes the end, and it will be fulfilled. If it seems slow in coming, wait patiently, for it will surely take place. It will not be delayed." (Habakkuk 2:2-3, NLT)

God seems to be saying to us: *The problem isn't that I don't have a vision for you; the problem is that you don't remember the vision I gave you. You need to write down that vision and you need to make it plain that anyone can carry it out so that in the midst of a corrupt society you can transform it.*

We are called to make His vision available to everyone, so that everyone can understand and receive it.

Revelation: The Power to Transform

Vision is a revelation of God's heart for mankind, a revelation for you and those around you. The word vision in Hebrew (chazon) has, as a part of its meaning, the word revelation embedded in it. In fact, some translations of the Bible say without vision people have no discipline and no boundaries.

God's vision is so powerful; full of possibility and rich with potential, it can change you and the world. Just as with Habakkuk, it can transform cities and nations. It can affect our marriages, our families, our health, and everything else because His vision brings order, grace, and purpose.

---

30 Habakkuk 1:2-4

Your Assignment

Now you know there is only one vision for mankind, but there are many assignments. Each assignment is a role, a responsibility. Your assignment is your role in God's vision.

The church you belong to has a role. Your family and your city have one too, because God's vision encompasses everyone. Each of these people and groups get to carry out a portion, an assignment, of the overall vision of God.

You're probably thinking, aren't we supposed to be talking about money here?. What does money have to do with my assignment? With this revelation from God? With this Covenant? What does my money have anything to do with a sleepy Abraham and his old pregnant wife?

As it turns out...a lot.

WEALTH

First, let's define wealth. Are you picturing King Midas sitting on top of a pile of gold? Is there an emperor with vast amounts of land and power?

According to Merriam-Webster, the definition of wealth is this:

> *An abundance of valuable material possessions or resources.*[31]

The urban dictionary is similar but adds an important nuance:

> *Controlling and possessing money or personal property.*[32]

---

[31] wealth Def. 2. *Merriam-Webster.com.* (2017) Retrieved January 8, 2017, from https://www.merriam-webster.com/dictionary/wealth.
[32] wealth. top definition. Urbandictionary.com (2017). Retrieved January 8, 2017, from www.urbandictionary.com/define.php?term=wealth

Whether specifying an element of control or not, though, both definitions stress the same thing: Wealth is valued literally in money.

Money has a storied past.[33] We think of it as coins and bills because it has looked like that for a long time – certainly during our lifetime. But ancient African and American civilizations, tired of the cumbersome transactions of exchanging not-pocket-friendly cattle, traded shells as currency. By about 3000 BC Egypt and Mesopotamia were valuing money in gold bars and those bars would eventually be made into smaller, portable versions like jewelry and coins that could be traded more easily. This was also a way for people to keep an eye on their wealth at all times.

The Bible talks a lot about money. It reminds us that God cares about you.

By the time the 18th century BC rolled around, Babylonian priests were keeping watch over, and making loans from, the gold that was stored in the temple. This is where modern-day banking found its first roots. Fast forward forty centuries or so, and we still use banks to deposit, withdraw, and make loans today. It is the central system used to move money from place to place. Mind you, most money today is just paper no longer backed by gold. However we still place a monetary value on property and assets and exchange money for them all the time.

In the 21st century we sometimes use money and wealth colloquially as in, "I am rich in friends" or "I am going to invest my time." But wealth in God's economic system, as it relates to fulfilling the promise he made to Abraham, means actual money or its equivalent like land, property, treasures and assets.

33 Gascoigne, B. (2001). History of Money. Historyword.net. Retrieved from: http://www.historyworld.net/wrldhis/PlainTextHistories.asp?historyid=ab14

So while I wholeheartedly advise you to invest in both your relationships and your time management, that's not what we're talking about here. Money means...well...it means money.

Wealth: God is Going To Use It

The Bible talks a lot about money. It reminds us God cares about you and your finances and He has a plan for them that will require some wisdom and strategy.

If you ever want to look for wisdom and strategy for just about anything, the Bible is an interesting place to start. The Book of Deuteronomy, in particular, is rich in directives. At the time the book was being written, the Israelites were waiting to go into the promised land. Moses wanted to remind them where they'd come from, where they were going, and how they were going to get there. Deuteronomy is basically a collection of reminders to the people. It is in this just-pre-promised-land context that we revisit the Abrahamic Covenant:

"You shall remember the Lord your God, for it is He who gives you power to get wealth, that He may establish his covenant which He swore to your fathers, as it is this day." (Deuteronomy 8:18, NKJV)

There is only one over-arching purpose for wealth and that is to establish and confirm the Abrahamic Covenant. All wealth in the world, regardless of who controls it, has this singular purpose. Knowing His purpose for our finances keeps our hearts in alignment and it protects us as we steward what we've been given. You might ask, "What about my needs?" Money can be used to meet needs but that is not its purpose at all (more on that later). God's specific purpose in giving you the power to create wealth is not necessarily to give you a specific net worth but rather to empower you to participate in His vision. The more you deliberately align your finances with His vision, the more of God's wealth you will be entrusted with. If you apply these principles you will grow in finances, but it isn't for you to hoard or collect money just for the purpose of handling it, feeling secure in it, or passing it along. God's economy is for God's purpose.

In order to understand how God uses money to accomplish His purpose, we are going to dive a little bit deeper into the eighth chapter of Deuteronomy.

We just read that God promised to bring Israel into a time of prosperity. He promised they would have so many houses and so much food and clothing that they would be full in all ways, lacking in nothing. He also says, "You will bless the Lord your God for the good land he has given you."[34]

Beginning in verse 11, we get to the heart of the matter.

"But that is the time to be careful! Beware that in your plenty you do not forget the Lord your God and disobey his commands, regulations, and decrees that I am giving you today. For when you have become full and prosperous and have built fine homes to live in, and when your flocks and herds have become very large and your silver and gold have multiplied along with everything else, be careful!" (Deuteronomy 8:11-13, NLT)

God was saying, "So here's how this is going to work once you are wealthy." He is ok with you having beautiful houses and multiplying your cattle and your flocks. And while we certainly have beautiful houses today, not many of us are in the market for cattle and flocks. But we would have been in that day. In that day, this meant their businesses were multiplying.

Isn't it interesting that God wants your business to multiply? Or even, with all of the God things that He has going on, that He seems to be in the multiplication business? He seems ok with our silver, gold, houses, and overall assets multiplying. There must be a catch, though, right?

---

34 Deuteronomy 8:10

God can't mean that He wants us to sit around with a bunch of cash and count it. He doesn't.

Verse 14 continues:

"Do not become proud at that time and forget the Lord your God, who rescued you from slavery in the land of Egypt. Do not forget that he led you through the great and terrifying wilderness with its poisonous snakes and scorpions, where it was so hot and dry. He gave you water from the rock! He fed you with manna in the wilderness, a food unknown to your ancestors. He did this to humble you and test you for your own good." (Deuteronomy 8:14-16, NLT)

GOD HAS A PURPOSE AND MONEY FOLLOWS THAT PURPOSE

Here is a critical point: God is meeting their needs – He's saying our source of trust and sustenance is His promise and His word, not by anything else.

God's intention, always, is to do you good in the end.

Verses 17 and 18 bring us back to how wealth ties into this whole promise. The covenant referenced below is the Abrahamic Covenant.

"He did all this so you would never say to yourself, 'I have achieved this wealth with my own strength and energy.' Remember the Lord your God. He is the one who gives you power to be successful, in order to fulfill the covenant he confirmed to your ancestors with an oath." (Deuteronomy 8:17-18, NLT)

We are reaping the benefits of the Abrahamic Covenant even today. Jesus said:

But seek first the kingdom of God and His righteousness, and all these things shall be added to you." (Matthew 6:33 NKJV)

Later we will talk much more about the specific principles of multiplication, provision, and the resultant economy of a perfectly executed vision. But right now the thing to remember is simply this:

God's vision is for His purpose, and the purpose of wealth is to establish God's vision. Jesus says this same thing: seeking the kingdom is seeking God's vision. It you align with God's vision, money will serve you. But if you don't, money will rule over you. You'll be a slave.

God's vision is good. And it frees us.

Wealth: Generating Freedom

A Vision Statement Generator is a real thing. It's an online tool that combines nouns, verbs, and adjectives with some of your company's chosen key words and voila!—it spits out a vision statement in 30 seconds. I don't recommend it for several reasons, but mostly for this one: it's useless. What it writes sounds corporate speak-ish, but for the most part it is meaningless nonsense.

Bad vision statements offer no inspiration, no energy, and no direction. They give us a false sense of security.

Jesus says that if we seek first the Kingdom and align with its vision we will have everything we need. What does this mean? Does this mean God will deliver money onto the doorstep of the faithful and not of the unfaithful? Can we look at others' houses and ascertain whether or not they are aligning with God's vision? Not really.

He has promised to meet our needs, but notice that it's a promise.

It doesn't say "work and worry and fight endlessly for your needs to be met." It says He will meet our needs. Period. In fact, He says that by allowing him to meet our needs, we are free to trust God, free to seek contentment in God's purpose, and free to pursue righteousness, godliness, faith, love, steadfastness, and gentleness. We get outside of our own economy that binds us and into His economy that sets us free.

SOME ASSEMBLY REQUIRED

IKEA knows that most of the people walking through its doors are going to look for cheap furniture that still allows them to have self-respect. IKEA has a simple vision and it trusts that everyone from its distributors to its customers to its employees will understand it. By pricing merchandise inexpensively and making the shopping experience pleasant, IKEA makes sure everyone understands why they make furniture the way they do.

God's vision, once you catch it, is easy to understand, too. It is to establish and confirm the Abrahamic Covenant, and to fulfill this by blessing all people of the world through the person of Jesus Christ. And as we are reminded in Deuteronomy, God is going to give us the power to get wealth in order to move this Covenant to fulfillment.

Vision is necessary, but it must also be good. And God's vision –and His Covenant– are good. They are perfect. He made a pretty big promise and it includes every one of us. No strings attached.

We don't need to have twelve tribal sons or expect a geriatric pregnancy. We don't need to move to the promised land of the Old Testament, though we could if we wanted to. We don't have to do anything except align ourselves with our assignment in the great big vision of God.

If you think the story about how God uses money for His purpose is going to be filled with boring, pious Bible characters, cold checklists and stressful, divisive language that is incongruent with faith, think again. Abraham's mind was changed through vision. And that was just the beginning.

God may be about to change our minds, too.

CHAPTER 2

CHANGING OUR MINDS:
MONEY IN ITS PROPER PLACE

"A wise man should have money in his head, but not in his heart."
Jonathan Swift

This week I learned that pizza beach balls, collapsible pet dishes, and avocado tree starter kits were the top three trends I had apparently missed on Amazon.[1] And while I did not find myself aligning with Canadian shoppers' excitement over pepperoni-laced inflatables, I did take note that I was privy to this information in the first place. I know these things because my news feeds are filled with shortcuts purporting education, success, or happiness on nearly every topic imaginable. It didn't take very long to land upon my avocado-inclusive list.

If you spend more than half an hour per day on the Internet, chances are you will find checklists of every kind: 10 ways to be a good public speaker, this year's 25 best movies, 5 steps to developing a winning team, and 100 recipes you can make with five ingredients. Curious about the most soothing dog shampoo? There's a list for that, too. We are used to how-to lists.

So we gather our inspirational lists and our motivational videos. We buy our books and our treadmills and then we run on them, both proverbially and literally. Since we have more instant, yet questionably useful, information at our disposal than ever before

---

1   Aspler, S. (2017). 15 Products That Are Trending On Amazon Canada. Buzzfeed, Inc. Retrieved from: https://www.buzzfeed.com/sarahaspler/cool-products-canadians-are-buying-on-amazon-right-now?utm_term=.xr9XbE14o#.oxZVMeogZ

("How Many Of These Foods Taste Better With Mayo?"[2]), we rely more and more heavily on how to get more clicks, more followers, more likes, and more of everything. After a while we hit a wall.

It's easy to get addicted to the pursuit, a process that is robbing us from the focus of what we are working toward in the first place.

GETTING OUR HEAD IN THE GAME

We need a new mindset.

Have you ever been on a diet, trained for a race, studied for a PhD, or started a new business? If so, you know you can't make it happen with sheer willpower. You certainly can't make it happen overnight. Information itself does not make something happen for you. You can't read the right books, listen to the best podcasts or check boxes off the right lists to take you all the way to the finish line. But while you need a goal in sight and behavior that supports you as you work, you also need the heart and the mind to keep you going, indefinitely, even when things get rough.

To change your mindset you need inspiration. You save for an engagement ring because love is the motivator. You purchase the right equipment with the goal of climbing a mountain and not being the one lagging behind. You invest in a college education with the hope of a career that is a good fit for who you were created to be. We consider these things worth the expense because we have reason to trust that the money is going to do its job. It's going to fund our future—a future we have already bought into.

However, while we must put in the miles, the hours at work, or the deposits into savings that may not be enough. Eventually we burn out. You blow out your knee and the recovery is long. Or

---

2   Briceno, N. (2017). How Many of These Food Taste Better With Mayo? Buzzfeed, Inc. Retrieved from: https://www.buzzfeed.com/norbertobriceno/mayo-or-nayo?utm_term=.ry4N18e3g#.wqN63vXPM

there's a new manager who is insistent that you are not part of the new picture. Or there's a downturn in the economy and you don't have enough in savings to sweat it out until the upturn. Eventually something interrupts the momentum. And while self-discipline and action are very important, you can't behave all the way to a new mindset. You also need a change of heart. You can't change your mind without it.

Change your heart. Change your mind.

It's easy to exchange steak for ramen noodles when your heart is making the decisions. If money is making the decisions, your heart doesn't know what it wants.

If you desire, trust and pursue money in your heart, you will have money in your head. If you have it in your head, you'll look to it for inspiration. If you look to it to motivate, it will eventually hit a snag, and it will require more and more of you and take everything you have. You will be left wanting for more.

Why?

We forget that money is just a tool. It's a tool we use. It's a tool God uses, too. Money is simply a means of exchanging one thing for another and it can't be confused with the thing we are willing to exchange it for. It represents what we create, grow, fix, cook, teach, preach and eat. It is a means to defend, heal and care for the people we love. It's paper. It's coins. It moves about, but is never lost. And your money and heart will follow each other on the journey.

Your heart and your money are constant traveling companions. Where your money goes, your heart will follow.[3]

And if we aren't careful, our hearts will fail to realize that money can be a liar.

---

3 Matthew 6:21

TELLING THE TRUTH

We have become so culturally accustomed to hyperbolic speech that many of us have applied this posture of extremes to money, too. Save it all? Spend it all? Sell it all? Minimalism? The world wants us to take a pick and stand in a camp.

Our culture is filled with money's materialistic ability to provide everything. It's easy to obsess over trying to meet our own needs with money or hope to wield power with it. For some it's simply about seeking happiness.

Maybe we have discovered it's not the solution to everything, so we insist it's the root of all evil.

The love of money is the root of evil[4] for sure, but going without money isn't the opposite of evil.

The God of the Abrahamic Covenant offers a distinct mindset about money that focuses our hearts and heads toward one goal. It aligns our motivations with His purpose. And it corrects the voices that tell us either that we must be rich or we should be poor, and that our self-worth is derived from either one. It sets us free from the lies.

OLD MINDSET, OLD LIES: GOING TO EXTREMES

Before we take a look at this new mindset, I want to briefly address some of the evil, earthly ones.

The Lie of Wealth

The lie of wealth is that money is the most important thing there is. You may not think you believe this lie. Your initial reaction to this may be horror: Of COURSE I don't think money is the

---

4 I Timothy 6:10

most important thing there is. But consider this: whether little or much, we exchange it for everything all the time. We can't function without it.

The resulting problem is that we try to meet our own needs by trusting in money, desiring money, and pursuing money. We spend so much time doing these things that we enslave ourselves.

THE LOVE OF MONEY IS THE ROOT OF EVIL FOR SURE, BUT GOING WITHOUT MONEY ISN'T THE OPPOSITE OF EVIL.

We can even believe a lie about saving. We are bombarded with scary messages about having enough for retirement, education, and a possible downturn in our health. The truth is that as smart as saving is, trying to outrun any of those fears gets us outside of our purpose. When our money is focused on God's purpose and His vision, we are at peace.

The Lie of Poverty

If wealth does not satisfy and if the pursuit and love of money take our focus away from God's purpose, then the opposite must be true.

In other words…. Poverty is best, right?

Not really.

Mammon, the love of money and the belief that it will supply and satisfy your needs, is not part of God's economy. We will talk more about Mammon later but for now I want to point out that eschewing Mammon's economy is not equal to believing that poverty is the way to go. Valuing poverty itself is dysfunctional.

Doing so still places meaning in Mammon's money (in this case the value is in not having it) versus acknowledging that all money is God's and that we can trust how God is going to use it.

In your religious tradition you may have been taught the inherent value of poverty. This is a concept that has developed over centuries, but it is one without merit. Our Jewish ancestors, through whom we have the foundation of faith, felt the opposite: That to not enjoy material wealth was equal to not being grateful. Incidentally, you will never hear a Jew, or a Muslim for that matter, mention that God wants us to be poor.

St. Francis was famous for his vow of poverty. To him, and to his followers, poverty was the way of Jesus. Jesus, he claimed, was directly asking us to be poor. In fact, he made the analogy that we should pursue poverty with devotion equal to that of a man pursuing a beautiful woman. The ideal woman, and the one whom he chose to marry, was named "Lady Poverty."[5]

The vow of poverty was a concept born through monastic traditions and was loosely based on Biblical concepts taken largely out of context.[6] It was part of a larger vow (including chastity and obedience) that guaranteed their salvation but not anyone else's. This is in direct contrast and opposition to the Abrahamic Covenant, which promised salvation for everyone through faith.

Martin Luther, originally a poverty-promising monk himself, would later kick off the Reformation. He denounced this double standard as part of the 95 Theses nailed onto the famous door in Wittenberg, Germany on October 31, 1517. A vow of poverty, he said, was just one more way for people to measure one person against another.[7] Like many other things that people use to compare themselves to each other, it led to corruption and a

---

5 admin. (2015). Lady Poverty. TheDailyMass.com. Retrieved from: http://www.thedailymass.com/lady-poverty/
6 Matthew 10:7-19, Luke 18:18-23
7 Lang, S. (1988). The Urge for Poverty. Christian History Issue 19.

hypocritical disorientation of the gospel.

The truth is, we don't live without money and it is hypocritical to pretend that we do.

Those who espouse a zero-sum way of living still say money is important all the time. Even if we never exchange literal money, we exchange goods and services and gifts. We use resources of some kind and trade something of some value to procure what we want all the time.

The Lie of Being Unfit

One of the biggest lies we tell ourselves is that there is a merited aspect to money. We deserve it if we do well. If we believe that then we have to believe that the opposite is also true, that if we do something others would consider unwise with our money, we are bad and don't deserve it. In case we forget, our credit ratings, our bosses, and our neighbors are there to remind us if we are deserving or not. And if not then we are certainly unfit.

However according to the One who created us, we are anything but unfit. He has redeemed us and made us a fit in His eyes and for His plan. Our identity is defined by our heavenly Father and precedes the effective stewardship of money.

Money is just a tool. It comes and goes. But it never goes away—it just continues to change hands. Our self-worth is not tied to it either way. Money is just one thing that gets used to accomplish another.

The Lie of The Religious Mindset

It's easy for religious institutions and churches to reinforce the wrong thing too, for instance, that being poor is holy. Remember the vow of poverty? This hypocritical religious mindset wasn't just the monks' problem. Jesus confronted the religious elite of

His day and exposed the true motivations of their heart.

"The Pharisees, who dearly loved their money, heard all this and scoffed at him." (Luke 16:14, NLT)

They pretended like they didn't care about money and that they didn't want to talk about it, but meanwhile they loved it[8].

It's ironic that so many Christians talk about financial freedom as one thing: freedom from debt. There are followers of Christ who espouse financial principles rooted in working your fingers to the bone at all cost because God wants you free of debt. Getting rid of debt is not a bad idea. Being enslaved to it is tiresome and burdensome. However, working three jobs so you can buy a car with cash does not make you free. It does, however, give you something to brag about. There is nothing we do for ourselves that is better than what God provides for us.

God's blessing makes life rich; nothing we do can improve on God." (Proverbs 10:22, The Message)

The Hebrew text of this verse specifies that God's blessing is free of toil and sorrow. When our focus is wrong about finances we try to control the Church with money. This mindset brings the world's system into the church and attempts to make it function in God's economy. Instead, we should be taking God's system from within the Church and making it work in the world's economy. Leveraging for personal gain is a symptom of the world's economy and creates a dysfunctional religious hybrid. This sends us off course right away, even if it has God's name attached to it.

In other words, the religious mindset says: It's God's money, but with strings attached.

- I will give you money for your program if you let me sit on the board.

---

8 Matthew 23:1-33

- I will help you build the new children's wing, but I'll be right here waiting for a seat on the committee when you go searching for a new pastor. I want to donate a large amount to your evangelism campaign but then will have a lot to say about the music because as a major investor I of course have a weighted voice.

We need to reach the world, yes, but once we try to control the pastor or vision, we come under Mammon's system and its all over.

We need a new way of thinking about money. Why? Because God has said quite clearly that he is going to use it for a specific purpose. Having said that, looking for Jesus in a materialistic world can be difficult.

Working three jobs so you can buy a new car with cash does not make you free. It does, however, give you something to brag about.

NEW ECONOMY: NEW MIND

So we need to understand God's perspective on money. While the idea of God's system sounds so separate that we will need to do something weird and unfamiliar, it doesn't mean that at all. God's system doesn't cancel out the regular banking and financial systems that we are used to, or the ancient Egyptians were used to, or your grandparents may have used. God's economy works across many spectrums because it isn't separate. God's economy is one economy operating inside another. It's a different mindset.

While it isn't evil to participate in the world's economy, there is still a directive here: Be in it, but not of it. Participate in the world's system. That's fine, but function with a heavenly perspective inside of that worldly economy. Let that be what drives you from within.

What does this mean and how do we do it? Wrap your mind around this and sink it deep into your heart:

Money is just as much spiritual as it is natural.

Dual Citizenship: Money is Natural and Spiritual

Money has three components: first physical money or electronic money used for transactions. Second, the system that governs it. And third, the spirit connected to and supporting it. Money interacts with the spirit realm as much as it does with the physical realm. In ancient times gold was deposited and stored in temples under the stewardship of Egyptian and Babylonian priests. As mentioned before, by 1800 BC the Babylonian priests were making loans against the gold in these temples. Notice how Babylonian priests were entrusted with the economy of the day. This spiritual connection was not coincidental.

> **Money is just as much spiritual as it is natural.**

Money is governed by an economy—either God's or Mammon's—and it weaves its way through the spiritual realm and the earthly realm at the same time. God's economy is actually the economy of His Kingdom, and just as the Kingdom is invisible but functions in the world so does its economy. The earth and all its gold, silver, and assets are owned by God but it is not all under His management at the moment.[9]

God made us spiritual beings. He created us in His own image, intact with emotions, intellect, and creativity. He gave us each a

---

9 Psalm 24:1, Haggai 2:8

conscience. Genesis tells us he literally breathed life into us,[10] the same term used when the Holy Spirit is breathed into the New Testament believers.[11] We are created with a spirit and we are led by the Spirit.[12]

However, God didn't just make us spiritual beings; He also made us physical ones. We have physical bodies and live on physical land and operate inside of physical laws of science. We are dual citizens.

Your body is both natural and spiritual because your body is needed to affect heaven on earth. You have dual citizenship in both.[13] We are not ethereally moving about in space with no purpose. We are aligning our physical lives with our spiritual purpose. We decide what to put into our bodies, where we will live, and what we will do with our time. It all points to what our spirit values and says to us.

Money, too, is as spiritual as it is natural. Money moves through your reality with you. The Gospel of Matthew says our hearts follow our money:

"Wherever your treasure is, there the desires of your heart will also be." (Matthew 6:21, NLT)

Remember Deuteronomy 8:18? God didn't say he would give us power to do miracles, signs, and wonders through glory, love, gifts or holiness. As important as those other things are, He said He would use wealth. In other words, He cannot fulfill or confirm His Covenant – He cannot keep His promise – without wealth.

We use money. We need money. We have the power to get money. And God has said that, despite our inclination to trust in its inherent value, He will use it in invaluable ways to fulfill that which is of ultimate worth.

---

10 Genesis 2:7
11 John 20:22
12 Romans 8:14
13 1 Corinthians 15:46

God has said He needs to use wealth. This also means He will give you the power to get it. That's a big statement. Does that mean God wants you, for your own purposes, to be wealthy? No. By the same token, if God is giving you the power to get wealth, can this make money evil? No. It's the love of money and trust in it that is evil. We are asked to inhabit God's mindset here.

We are asked to know the purpose for wealth in our lives and never forget it. The purpose is to establish the Abrahamic Covenant and bless all families of the earth through the gospel of Jesus Christ and His Kingdom.

This Kingdom of God and its economy is accessible in the real world. We just have to learn how to function in it by applying its principles. When you do, you will notice an invisible blessing on you with tangible results in the real world for the greater good.

What we do on earth, including how and where we use our money, converts to spiritual action. What we do and say leaves the earthly realm and enters the heavenly realm. Once our actions, including how we use our money, leave the natural world and enter the spiritual world, a deposit is made into an account with our name on it and from this spiritual account we can make withdrawals.

"Don't store up treasures here on earth, where moths eat them and rust destroys them, and where thieves break in and steal. Store your treasures in heaven, where moths and rust cannot destroy, and thieves do not break in and steal." (Matthew 6:19-20, NLT)

You will notice your heavenly account is inflation-proof, theft-proof, and fireproof, and its dividends pay into the future. God is redeeming the world's economy through His system of investing in the Kingdom, just like He redeemed us out of the world and then places us in it for His purpose. He also is redeeming the wealth of this world and entrusting us with its necessary stewardship as we direct it towards His vision.

Clearly there is nothing divine about money that can be exchanged to buy us a bar of soap. It's fine—and the people sitting next to us in a meeting, on the train or at our dinner table undoubtedly appreciate that we've thought of it. However, God has bigger plans for money than just meeting our needs. Here's what God says:

Money has a divine signature, voice and destination.

"Come quickly now, you rich who lack true faith and hoard and misuse your resources, weep and howl over the miseries, the woes and judgments, that are coming upon you. Your wealth has rotted and is ruined and your fine clothes have become moth-eaten. Your gold and silver are corroded, and their corrosion will be a witness against you and will consume your flesh like fire. You have stored up your treasure in the last days when it will do you no good.

Look! The wages that you have fraudulently withheld from the laborers who have mowed your fields are crying out against you for vengeance; and the cries of the harvesters have come to the ears of the Lord of Heaven's Armies." (James 5:1-4, Amplified)

Notice in the above text money has a voice that is giving judicial testimony against its abusers. Money cries out when it is misdirected which means it is aware of its assignment and destination. Money is saying: "I'm being used for a purpose I wasn't designed for and in the hands of the wrong person. I am reserved for the stewards of God's economy please reassign me" Since money has a voice and an audience with God, it must be spiritual.

Judicial judgment is not because of the money itself, but is a result of pursuing our own desires while doing harm to others. The cries of the people you have cheated have reached the ears of the Lord of Heaven's Armies. Your favorite sweater has bugs chewing holes in it for dinner. Your jewelry is turning your skin green. Your flesh is on fire. Yikes.

"Money talks" is an aphorism that has definitely earned its staying power. And it has been talking for a really long time. Let's continue to look at some examples of how money has a voice and interacts with the spirit realm.

This first story is about a couple of Old Testament sons with some sacrifices. And the second is about a couple of guys busy buying food for the poor and managing herds of animals dancing in God-synchronized New Testament dreams.

Abel

We all know about Adam and Eve. Their likenesses are plastered on everything from medieval frescos to children's classrooms to Art Deco wine labels where Eve is usually portrayed as both seductive and guilty at the same time. She's nearly always holding an apple. Both she and her husband are always fancifully attired in the just-got-kicked-out-of-the-garden fig leaves.

Well, after their famous fruit-eating sin and its aftermath of hard labor and painful childbirth, they settled into a life of working the land and raising a family. And the first time out of the gate they got a two for one deal.

Cain and Abel, the sons of Adam and Eve, knew their parents' history with God Almighty. To show their allegiance to His power over their lives, they offered some of the first recorded sacrifices in the Bible. Cain kept the best for himself and offered God his second-best. But God rejected them, which did not make Cain happy. Abel leaned on the grace of God and brought something he wasn't responsible for growing: the blood of an animal. He brought the first and one of the best animals he had and he sacrificed it. And his offering was made by faith. God seemed to be pleased with this.[14]

So in a fit of jealous rage, Cain killed Abel.

---

14 Genesis 4:2-7

However, death could not silence his sacrifice.

"It was by faith that Abel brought a more acceptable offering to God than Cain did. Abel's offering gave evidence that he was a righteous man, and God showed his approval of his gifts. Although Abel is long dead, he still speaks to us by his example of faith." (Hebrews 11:4, NLT)

This seems random except that what Abel's offering was saying would be important to a future Abraham, the rest of the Old Testament prophets, and the Messiah who would later come. It would serve as a mouthpiece.

Abel's offering became a voice. We still hear it today.

Abel's offering was still speaking to New Testament believers as to what would be the way of the cross. The cross would require blood and faith. It would require sacrifice. It would require faith that God was still in the process of bringing to fulfillment the Covenant that He promised. Abel trusted for God to provide his needs. Thousands of years after Abel died, the measure of his faith and offering still is heard across all of history.

Cornelius

Abel's offering still speaks and this became the case for a first century centurion named Cornelius.[15]

Cornelius was a Roman army officer, a captain of the Italian Regiment. He feared God, prayed regularly, and gave generously to the poor. He was also a Gentile.

Being a Gentile is significant here. Remember that the gospel hadn't spread to the Gentiles yet. Technically, Cornelius was not one of the chosen people. He was not Jewish. But by giving generously to the poor – by unwittingly allowing for God to provide their needs through him – he was channeling his money

---

15 Acts 10:1-8

to do the work of God. He was making deposits into a heavenly account that he didn't yet know he had, although that was about to change. In fact, everything was about to change.

Remember how God likes to tell people things in visions?

One afternoon an angel appeared to Cornelius in a vision and said,

"Your prayers and gifts to the poor have been received by God as an offering!" (Acts 10:4, NLT)

The next day, the apostle Peter had a vision, too. Remember Peter? He was a fisherman. He tried walking on water. He once cut off a guy's ear. He was one of the twelve apostles and, though somewhat impulsive and unpredictable, was one of Jesus' closest friends. Jesus' death, burial, and resurrection were likely still fresh in Peter's mind when he had this vision.

Peter's vision was a bit more cinematic than Cornelius'. In fact, the Bible calls it a trance. In this vision, Peter saw a sheet descend from heaven and on it were all sorts of animals, birds, and reptiles. God told Peter to eat whatever animals he wanted.

Why did this matter? Peter was confused. Up to this point he would not have been allowed, by Jewish custom, to eat any animal that was considered unclean. But now God was telling him, so it seemed, "Oh I don't care about that anymore! I have made everything clean so help yourself!" (This vision repeated three times.) As soon as this happened, the sheet and its Zootopia went back up into heaven and Peter came out of the vision.[16]

As he sat scratching his head, contemplating the meaning of the vision, three men appeared at his door. "Cornelius the Centurion has sent for you," the men said to Peter. So they all headed off to Cornelius' house together. When they arrived, there was an expectant gathering of people, waiting for what Peter was going

---

16 Acts 10:9-16

to say to them. Here's what he said:

"You know is against our laws for a Jewish man to enter a Gentile home like this or associate with you. But God has shown me that I should no longer think of anyone as impure or unclean. So I came without objection as soon as I was sent for. Now tell me why you sent for me." (Acts 10:28-29, NLT)

Well, this is weird, he thought. We were both visited in visions at the same time? Cornelius replied:

Four days ago I was praying in my house about this same time, three o'clock in the afternoon. Suddenly, a man in dazzling clothes was standing in front of me. He told me, Cornelius, your prayer has been heard, and your gifts to the poor have been noticed by God! Now send messengers to Joppa, and summon a man named Simon Peter....Now we are all here, waiting before God to hear the message the Lord has given you." (Acts 10:30-33, NLT)

Cornelius gave money to the poor and it testified to God. Do you hear that? The money itself spoke to God.

But what happened when the money spoke?

Later, Peter and Cornelius compared visions. Peter's vision clearly told him that God showed no favoritism, that Jews and Gentiles were both worthy of the gospel now. They were filled with the Holy Spirit[17] and Peter and those accompanying him water baptized Cornelius and his household right then and there. The baptism of the Gentiles became a game changer.

Cornelius' gift to the poor spoke to God and got His attention. By giving, Cornelius made room for God's vision and God made room for Cornelius in His vision. His prayer and money opened the door for the gospel to be available to the Gentiles, making room for them in God's vision, too. And from then on, the gospel of Christ, the Messiah promised through the Covenant of

---

17 Acts 10:44-48

Abraham, would now be available to everyone, everywhere.

It is still available to everyone, everywhere, today.

Breaking Open The Alabaster Box

The story of Cornelius centers on a couple of men who were visited by God in visions. This next one is about a visit, too. It's about a woman this time and she was visiting none other than Jesus himself.

Jesus had a habit of hanging out with the least likely people, and this time it was with a man named Simon, who was a leper. While Simon and Jesus were eating, a woman walked in with a jar of expensive perfume and she did the most bizarre thing. She broke it – and then poured it over Jesus' head. People at the table were indignant. But Jesus foretold the goodness of this decision:

"Leave her alone. Why criticize her for doing such a good thing to me? You will always have the poor among you, and you can help them whenever you want to. But you will not always have me. She has done what she could and has anointed my body for burial ahead of time. I tell you the truth, wherever the Good News is preached throughout the world, this woman's deed will be remembered and discussed." (Mark 14:6-9, NLT)

Socially, this was a faux pas on several levels. She was a woman, for one. Which means she wasn't supposed to be the center of attention. Second, she broke something valuable – which seemed careless. She wasted an entire container of expensive perfume by dumping it over Jesus' head, which appears to be overly emotional and irresponsible. Remember that unhealthy religious system? It can tend to value carefulness, reserve and responsibility, and the pursuit of holiness through rules and regulations over something deeper.

Jesus didn't care about any of those things. He cared about the heart. To begin with, He valued women. And all of the fuss over her not being careful, responsible and emotionally stable at all times: those are things we care about. Jesus didn't. In fact, He thought so highly of what she did that He said we would never forget it.

It's the 21st century and we haven't forgotten it yet. Her gift became a voice testifying of Jesus' death even until today.

There is a thread of faith that binds these stories together both to their past and their future.

" All these people earned a good reputation because of their faith, yet none of them received all that God had promised. For God had something better in mind for us, so that they would not reach perfection without us." (Hebrews 11:39-40, NLT)

What does this mean?

Some of the heroes of our Christian faith certainly saw some promises come to pass. But they didn't see eternal life as promised because the Messiah would not be realized in their lifetime. God seemed to have in mind that the fulfillment of the promise to Abraham would be in us, the New Testament believers. The Old Testament and New Testament believers would both experience the reward of faith in the future: the promise of eternal life.[18]

So God uses money in unique ways by assigning it a divine signature, voice, and destination. And He listens to this voice, even today.

Many have yet to be blessed by the Abrahamic Covenant and God's vision. Our mindset toward money has a surprising amount to do with it.

A War Over Wealth

So why didn't God promise to confirm His Covenant by using

---

18 Matthew 27:53

love, glory, and gifts? Why did He promise to use wealth? Wealth is important because it can interact with the spirit realm every time it changes hands and moves about. If you don't understand wealth you will not fully be able to establish His Covenant.

Money functions either under the command of Mammon—the CFO of Satan's kingdom—or God—the Lord of Heaven's Armies. His armies of heavenly helpers are always deployed wherever money is moving. That's why there's a great war over the minds of people and their finances. Satan works overtime to get the hearts and minds of people in the religious tradition to believe that God wants them to be poor. It's a stronghold of Satan.

So where do we come in? We are to have a different mindset about money, and one that works within the regular, worldly system. As this change of heart and mind take place and our actions follow, money will move spiritually and physically at the same time back to the house of God to establish His vision.

And our job is to become stewards of it.

SACRED STEWARDSHIP

What is a steward?

Stewardship is management of someone else's wealth.[19] A steward is not given wealth to hoard it or build a fortress around it. Neither is the steward given it to be careless or self-serving. A steward is an asset manager. There is never a question of whose assets are being managed.

This is the whole mindset of the heavenly economy: We are stewards of someone else's – God's – money. And our mindset toward money in both the physical and spiritual sense will turn our heart to God. Stewardship allows us to hold money with

---

19 stewardship. (2017). Merriam-Webster.com. Retrieved from: https://www.merriam-webster.com/dictionary/stewardship

open hands because it all belongs to Him.

This includes tithing and seed sowing. But it may also include real world economics such as investing. Do you have a knack for investing? Then invest! Use your gifts for God's glory. God created you with certain gifts and resources on purpose. Put them to use! It's all God's anyway.

Stewardship is described many places, but in the gospel of Luke Jesus offers some explanation by way of parables about some wealthy men.

Two Rich Guys, One Shady Manger, and a Bunch of Big Barns

Rich Man #1 made so much money that he had no more room to store all his possessions.[20] So he built more barns and storehouses and he spent his free time admiring them, and feeling safe in them. But God was disgusted with this. Why? It wasn't because he was rich. God doesn't seem to care about that. It's because he was not rich in God's economy. His trust was in his possessions. His worry about them made him unable to think of his money spiritually and to entrust God to use it.

STEWARDSHIP KEEPS MONEY FROM BECOMING A COMPETING GOD.

Jesus' point? The problem is not the money itself but our trust in it. That is what changes our focus and when our trust is in money, our focus is on *us*. When we trust in money rather than God, the money misses its purpose in our life.

Part of this new era of Jesus is a commitment to others, and

---

20 Luke 12:13-21

stewardship is part of that. If you're trustworthy in managing money (your own or someone else's), then you can be entrusted with the more important things.

The Rich Man and The Dishonest Manager

Enter Rich Man #2 Rich guy #2 employed a financial manager who was not all that great at his job of being a financial manager.[21] When the rich man came looking for his money and found that the manager had been managing it poorly, he threatened to fire him. So the manager schemed a plan. He went around to all of the rich man's debtors and short-saled their debts.

"The manager thought to himself, "Now what? My boss has fired me. I don't have the strength to dig ditches, and I'm too proud to beg. Ah, I know how to ensure that I'll have plenty of friends who will give me a home when I am fired." (Luke 16:3-4, NLT)

This is a weird solution, selling debts for less than their face value, but not a culturally uncommon one at the time. The master was actually pleased with the manager's actions because he acted swiftly to prepare for his future.

If it seems incongruous for the master to be pleased that he had lost money, remember that it is a parable. Jesus is telling a bigger story than money management here.

Jesus was not praising the steward's management style. He was teaching about the shrewdness of the steward: he took advantage of his position to point to his future. If we had the same excitement and enthusiasm and work ethic toward God's vision that others have toward pursing pleasure and unrighteous wealth, how rich we would be!

"The rich man had to admire the dishonest rascal for being so shrewd. And it is true that the children of this world are

---
21 Luke 16:1-13

more shrewd in dealing with the world around them than are the children of the light. Here's the lesson: Use your worldly resources to benefit others and make friends. Then, when your possessions are gone, they will welcome you to an eternal home." (Luke 16:8-9, NLT)

The unjust steward was forward-thinking. Jesus is making an important point here: use your current resources to plan for eternity. What does this mean? It means whatever income you have, set your mind to God's purpose. When you invest your money in God's vision to redeem people and bring salvation you will be welcomed into their eternal homes. Jesus made it clear if we cannot steward the wealth of the world then we cannot be entrusted with the true riches, which is the souls of mankind, His glory, and the Kingdom.[22]

Stewardship keeps money from becoming a competing god.

So, how does the new mindset about money hold up to God's purpose for us? Let's compare.

Old Money Mindset:

- We need to figure money out.

- Money: it all belongs to us.

- We need to work and sweat and worry about how to get by. We need to decide if we are in the "God wants us to be rich" resort, or across the river in the campground of "God wants us to be poor." We need to be responsible with money in a worldly sense in order to please God. And if we keep looking and trying hard enough, we're going to find a solution for how to do all this.

---

[22] Luke 16:11

No treadmill, willpower, or checklist necessary.

New Money Mindset:

- God has already given us the solution.

- Money: It all belongs to God.

- It has a purpose and it is spiritual.

- God allows it to change hands and he allows it to speak.

- He is redeeming the economy.

- Money can be used for good or for evil and God gives us freedom to choose either.

- Our hearts will follow it wherever it goes, and both are called back to their destination, to the God they belong to.

- Wealth's purpose is to fulfill the Abrahamic Covenant.

- God's Covenant is part of His vision, which has promised redemption for all of us.

- We are stewards of words of eternal life.

No treadmill, willpower, or checklist necessary.

CHAPTER 3

SAFE:
THE FEAR FACTOR

*"Obstacles are those frightful things you see
when you take your eyes off your goal."*

Henry Ford

By the time the Ford Motor Company was founded in 1903, Henry Ford was on his third automobile business. He ended his workdays in a house illuminated by candlelight—a house that, powered by a friendship with Thomas Edison, he would later live to see lit by electricity. He started life traveling by horses and wagons and he ended it driving in cars. A lot of cars.

When Ford unveiled his first Model T in 1908, he was a busy man. He ran an efficient business that made an affordable, dependable product and he made a fortune by making one thing very well: a black Model T car. And he changed the course of history[1].

The scope of his business was far bigger than the Model T, though. Henry Ford changed the world by putting an assembly line in the heart of the car-building process. In addition to making cars more affordable, this jump-start to the Industrial Revolution went on to change nearly every industry.

He set a new standard of paying people well—double what most people were making at the time. And this change, in turn, gave him customers with enough money to afford his product. He was largely responsible for creating the American middle class. He even changed dating, shifting it from the front porch to the back

---

1 October 01 This Day In History. (2017). For Motor Company unveils the Model T. History.com. A&E Television Networks, LLC. Retrieved from: http://www.history.com/this-day-in-history/ford-motor-company-unveils-the-model-t

seat.[2] Couples were now on the move.

Henry's dreams for the future could be nearly endless because if he didn't know how to do something, he leaned heavily on the knowledge that someone else did. He had his own mastermind group.

> "Let me remind you that I have a row of electric buttons in my office. All I have to do is press one of them to call the person who can answer any question on any subject I wish to know, relative to the business at hand. I take care of the business, they take care of the questions."

Henry freed himself to do what he did well – his assignment was to run a successful business.

Henry went on to buy a railroad, a number of coal mines, a sawmill, a glassworks manufacturer, and even some South American rubber plantations. What came of this were nearly endless numbers of job opportunities. Not only were jobs created for men, but the demand for employment was so great, he pioneered new job opportunities for women and the disabled. His high wages and fight for employees' rights caught the world's attention. Other companies would very quickly follow suit.[3]

Like many of us, Henry eschewed change unless he launched it and grew to be fearful of what was out of his control. He feared the government, or at least the control of government over business. He distrusted Hollywood, new music, and most things that fell into the category of "things the kids do these days." He opposed social and cultural change that he didn't understand or value, and as he became more successful this led to an increased anxiety over others' intentions about his business.

Over the nearly two decades Henry was building Model Ts and amassing a tremendous amount of wealth, his fear was

---

2 Bailey, B. (1989). From Front Porch to Back Seat: Courtship in Twentieth-Century America. John Hopkins University Press.
3 Stanford, Steven. (2014). Henry Ford – An Impact Felt. Henry Ford Heritage Association. Retrieved from: http://hfha.org/the-ford-story/henry-ford-an-impact-felt/

growing, as well. As Ford became more hostile toward unions, immigration and competition, his unease with progress got him into some hot water. He turned a blind eye to those closest to him and a deaf ear to his own voice. The result was one bizarre conspiracy theory.

In response to information he was being fed by those closest to him, Henry took his thoughts to the newspaper-reading masses with articles claiming the Jews' plans for world domination. And much like we do when we get on social media with fingers ready to pounce by fashioning the rant of the century, he did so quite badly.

The articles claimed, at least by implication, Jewish responsibility for everything from World War I to the national debt to a manipulation of diplomacy in its entirety. He accused Jewish automobile dealers of conspiring to undermine Ford sales policies, which of course was really the heart of the matter. Ford let his fear think for him and when he started getting anxious about money, things got pretty weird.

While Ford would later claim that his thoughts published over a seven-year period in the newspaper were done so without his knowledge and as part of a conspiracy against him, there was no turning back the clock. When Jewish people began suing him over his audacious claims, Ford even faked a car accident (the irony) so that he could hide away in a hospital in hopes of avoiding having to testify at a trial.

When prominent Jewish leaders called for a boycott of Ford cars, money finally spoke back to Henry. He apologized for the misunderstanding, claiming himself a victim, too. He clarified that he had no knowledge of the contents of what was being published weekly, for seven years, under his name. Regardless of how these pieces came to be, though, they wouldn't have existed at all if Ford had just stuck to his vision and refused to listen to the voices that weren't speaking to it.[4]

Henry Ford had more than a great vision for his company; he had a vision for the future. For decades businesses would follow his example and try to emulate his core values of quality, service and ingenuity. He was inarguably successful and a business exemplar to those wishing to make money by doing one thing better than anyone else. But for all of the reasons to emulate him, his story also teaches us something else.

Fear Is a Liar

Be afraid. Be very afraid. This is the message.

Henry Ford didn't enjoy his journey because he didn't realize that even if you have an amazing impact, fear could rob you of your joy.

Today, when we sign into our bank accounts, bill pay programs, or the app that buys us songs for a dollar, we notice that the levels of security everywhere are going up. We now have two-step security, fingerprint authentication, and retina recognition. We have so much security that we find ourselves secure for security's sake.

Unfortunately, though, the reason we keep changing our passwords and adding our thumbprints is because we all know deep down inside that it isn't real. We aren't secure. Nothing is guaranteed. We put 9000 tags on our luggage and it still gets lost. Some people eat nothing but vegetables and still get cancer.

And yet – we chase it. We know we can't catch security but we keep running after it like there's a rabbit just out of reach in front and we are the dogs in desperate pursuit of some dinner.

---

[4] Anti-Semitism in the United States. (n.d.). Henry Ford Invents a Jewish Conspiracy. Jewish Virtual Library. Retrieved from: http://www.jewishvirtuallibrary.org/henry-ford-invents-a-jewish-conspiracy

We are afraid of money. We are afraid of being poor. We are afraid of being rich. We fear the sacrifices necessary to make money and the temptations available to us if we do. We fear the prosperity gospel but we fear the poverty one just as much. We are fearful because we are listening to the wrong voices.

Fear has a bad message. It wishes to keep us dependent. It has the ability to keep us safe, yes, but it is also a manipulative jerk. And for all of its promises, when it comes to its impact on our finances, the prospects are grim.

FEAR: AFRAID OF RAGS AND RICHES

Fear of Poverty

It's a nearly universal truth. We are afraid of not having enough money.

Whether you've experienced real poverty in your lifetime or not, we all understand the powerlessness that comes with not having enough money. Poor family systems, depression-era mentalities, and bad personal choices all contribute to the scarcity mindset that afflicts those of us who, by global standards at least, are actually rich.

Maybe you really have been afflicted by genuine poverty and this has motivated you to work even harder. And you work out of fear because you never want that to happen again. The fear of poverty is the very thing that keeps you from moving past it. You become a controller.

Regardless of your reasons, though, the danger of losing it all feels imminent and this has sent you running.

And now, fear controls you.

At different times in our lives, fear controls all of us. In the twelfth chapter of the Gospel of Luke, Jesus has some gracious words for us about why it shouldn't:

"Look at the ravens. They don't plant or harvest or store food in barns, for God feeds them. And you are far more valuable to him than any birds! Can all your worries add a single moment to your life? And if worry can't accomplish a little thing like that, what's the use of worrying over bigger things?

Look at the lilies and how they grow. They don't work or make their clothing, yet Solomon in all his glory was not dressed as beautifully as they are. And if God cares so wonderfully for flowers that are here today and thrown into the fire tomorrow, he will certainly care for you. Why do you have so little faith?

And don't be concerned about what to eat and what to drink. Don't worry about such things. These things dominate the thoughts of unbelievers all over the world, but your Father already knows your needs. Seek the Kingdom of God above all else, and he will give you everything you need." (Luke 12:24-31, NLT).

God has made a way for us to live free of the fear of being poor. Adhering to God's economy is, like other moral issues, a choice for us to make by faith. And choice is important here. Without it, economic morality would be compulsory, which would negate the need for grace.

Fear makes grace impossible because in trying to meet our own needs, even in part, we are no longer free. And if we are not free, we are not free to choose anything, including the gospel of Christ.

So the fear of poverty is common enough for most of us to relate to, but there's something else. There's also a fear of wealth. And I think more people suffer from it than we realize.

Fear of Being Rich

What is it that makes us reticent about wealth?

Corruption. We know inherently that love of money can create a mindset that brings greed and corruption, and we know this at every income level and at every age. This fear doesn't need for us to be wealthy or poor and is no respecter of cultural background.

In our earliest childhood, most of us remember fairy tales where the bad guy is a rich king trying to oppress our hero. We think of Robin Hood stealing from the rich to give to the poor, and we remember the castle on the hill is a symbol of domination, oppression and flying monkeys. Something deep within us has the sense that the person with all of the money will use it for evil.

We have this fear for good reason. The power that comes with wealth is real. If the person with the wealth has bad vision – or worse yet, has no vision at all – the results can be catastrophic.

Pride. We humans have been known to be prideful for very strange reasons. The religious spirit says there is value in being poor, that there is value in going off the grid, participating exclusively outside of an earthly banking system, and misunderstanding entirely that eye of the needle and the camel we try to shove through it.

In the Gospel of Mark, Jesus says this:

"And the disciples were astonished at His words. But Jesus answered again and said to them, "Children, how hard it is for those who TRUST[5] in riches to enter the kingdom of God! 25 It is easier for a camel to go through the eye of a needle than for a rich man to enter the kingdom of God." (Mark 10:24,25, NKJV)

Notice the disciple's response. They were astonished! Why? Because the Jewish mindset would be saying, "What? But what

---

5 Emphasis added.

about the Covenant? God promised wealth within His Covenant. Did something change?"

But they didn't get the point. Nothing changed. Jesus isn't asking us to be poor or saying that God isn't going to come through on His promise. He is simply asking us to desire, trust, and pursue Him rather than money. Trying to impress God with money is like shoving a camel through the eye of a needle because it distorts our priorities. However, desiring, trusting, and pursuing God while operating a heavenly economy inside of an earthly banking system realigns those priorities. It's an acknowledgment that in God we know we have everything we need.

Increased Responsibility. With wealth comes some risk. The risk of financial failure feels larger, as does the responsibility that comes along with it. Wealthy people are the targets of a certain type of hate and jealousy. And one wealthy person in a room, a group or a business incites a competitive environment that isn't always healthy and sometimes is downright scary. When good advice is given to a rich man it is hard to know whom to trust. It's hard to know who the real friends of a rich person really are.

To be honest, it's healthy to be somewhat concerned that money may not be all it's cracked up to be. Just before he speaks to us about worrying about too little money, Luke also speaks about what to do if you've got a lot of it:

"A person is a fool to store up earthly wealth but not have a rich relationship with God." (Luke 12:21, NLT).

Notice he doesn't say that having the money itself is wrong. He only speaks to priorities.

We have talked about the fear of each end of the financial spectrum – the threat of being poor and the dangers of trusting money without understanding wealth's purpose. But I want to address some of our other fear-related issues when it comes to money. I want to talk about the threat of temptation, sacrifice, and self-worth that our obsession with money gives to us. And then we're going to discuss what God wants us to do about it.

FEAR: AFRAID OF TEMPTATION

Let's face it. We are challenged by money and the system that governs it everywhere we go.

The next generation of students getting ready to graduate from high school and college have more money, less ambition, greater depression, and three times the teen suicide rate of the generation before it. We have easier to access to suburban drugs, fast cars that can be driven while under the influence of just about anything, and a culture that makes getting out of one "relationship" and into another by dinnertime an easy reality.

We have an undisputed addiction to buying and consuming and the law of diminishing returns rules over us. We keep spending and acquiring and wanting more but our happiness is less and less each time. So the next time we just buy more. And like any addiction, the cycle continues.

It's easy to blame the money itself. It's easy to fear that having more money will automatically make us more at risk for risky behavior. It's not the money's fault any more than it's McDonald's fault that we've gained 20 pounds this year. The wide variety of choices available for purchase at fast food restaurants is not making us fat and unhealthy. The wrong mindset toward it is.

It's the same with money. Whether rich or poor, money makes it easier for you to access things that can harm you. However, the freedom does not have to be overwhelming. It is the LOVE of money that is the problem, not the cash in your pocket.

"But people who long to be rich fall into temptation and are trapped by many foolish and harmful desires that plunge them into ruin and destruction. For the love of money is the root of all

kinds of evil." (I Timothy 6:9-10, NLT)

How can the love of money be the root of all evil? Let me explain it this way. There are three components of money: First, there is the money that you can hold in your hand. Second, there is a system to manage or govern it. And third, there is a spirit behind money and therefore loving it empowers that spirit.

So, if we love, trust, and pursue money, then money becomes our master. Money governs and we are enslaved by it. Just look at the evil schemes of drug and human traffickers, banking cartels and wars around the world and you will find all of them rooted in the love of money. Fear accompanies every form of slavery.

If we function within God's economy and desire, trust, and pursue Him we will have everything we need. When God is governing and in charge there is no fear.

In the Apostle Paul's first letter to Timothy, he encourages us not to be tempted by pride or to trust in our money:

"Teach those who are rich in this world not to be PROUD and not to TRUST in their money, which is so unreliable. Their trust should be in God, who richly gives us all we need for our enjoyment."[6] (I Timothy 6:17, NLT)

God is aware of temptation, too. And He's created you to withstand it.

"The temptations in your life are no different from what others experience. And God is faithful. He will not allow the temptation to be more than you can stand."(I Corinthians 10:13, NLT)

FEAR: AFRAID OF MISMANAGEMENT

Everything comes at a cost. The decision to part with your

---

6 Emphasis added

money comes with no small amount of consideration. There are even financial calculators to help you to determine the worth of a purchase, large or small.

- If I save the money I spend at Starbucks every day and instead make coffee at home, how much will I have saved in five years?

- If I buy a beat-up house in a great neighborhood, how much can I put into it to flip it for a substantial profit when the market recovers?

- How many phone calls, letters, or emails will it take to win a prospective client?

We are used to a cost/benefit ratio for everything. While we may be afraid to bite the bullet and invest our hard-earned cash, drink a slightly less satisfying cup of coffee, or send yet another email to our A-List clients, we are still usually clear on the goal: To save money, to make money, or to win business. We can measure it.

But what happens when this applies to giving? What if the cost/benefit test doesn't really work to my satisfaction because I can't "measure" its exact worth? The answer is: you don't. God's vision is that you depend on Him to provide. You give freely, out of the joy in your heart. You stop trying to leverage a formula and step into what has immeasurable potential.

FEAR: AFRAID OF UNCERTAINTY

With the need to provide food, clothing, and shelter for ourselves, and also to provide for our families, we live under the constant cloud of "What if?" What if our job changes? What if I don't have enough for retirement? What if this house ends up being a money pit and I lose money? What if I die young and don't leave enough to my children? What if I make a comfortable living and my children end up spoiled and without values?

This uncertainty is a bottomless pit. And when it comes to constantly pursuing, trusting in, and desiring more money, we find ourselves running faster, rather than slower toward an out-of-focus and just-out-of-reach goal.

Fear wishes to enslave us, knowing it can only do so if we forget or ignore that love makes us free. In the next chapter, we are going to examine how constantly driving to provide for ourselves is the opposite of what we have been asked to do.

Matthew, the first book of the New Testament, answers the question this way:

"If God gives such attention to the appearance of wildflowers – most of which are never even seen – don't you think he'll attend to you, take pride in you, do his best for you? What I'm trying to do here is to get you to relax, to not be so preoccupied with 'getting,' so you can respond to God's 'giving.'

People who don't know God and the way he works fuss over these things, but you know both God and how he works. Steep your life in God-reality, God-initiative, God-provisions. Don't worry about missing out. You'll find all your everyday human concerns will be met." (Matthew 6:30-33, MSG)

God says that fear of uncertainty and insecurity is unnecessary. It doesn't really matter. If you are aligning with what God is giving to you, if you are facing your fear with gratitude, then you will have all you need. Clothes. Food. Shelter. Literally all that you need.

FEAR: YOU ARE NOT ENOUGH

We have shown how fear leads us to spend money, to hoard money, to judge other people with too much or too little of it, and to make gods out of responsibility, security, and safety. But there is another layer here.

Sometimes the fear of not having enough is really a fear that you aren't enough.

We fear that we aren't strong enough to handle challenges. That we won't survive. That people will judge us. That we don't have enough faith. But Jesus has some things to say about this.

"Are not five sparrows sold for two copper coins?[a] And not one of them is forgotten before God. But the very hairs of your head are all numbered. Do not fear therefore; you are of more value than many sparrows" (Luke 12:6-7, NKJV)

The very hairs on your head are numbered.

You are more than enough.

Maybe when you started reading this book you shared some of these same fears. You were afraid of poverty, of being rich, and of the temptations that come alongside either. Perhaps you have been bogged down in the endless cycle of what ifs. It's very possible you are confusing not having enough with not being enough.

I would like to examine one more fear: The felt anxiety when money collides with the church. And while I want to talk about fear where it applies to church and religious culture, don't mistake "church" for God's economy. God's economy is larger. It operates in the world. It's an economy of the Kingdom that functions in this world, but is not separate from it.

That being said, let's specifically consider the church in general and why we are afraid that it wants our money.

SCARED: THE FEARFUL MARRIAGE OF CHURCH AND MONEY

If you've spent any time in church, you know that Murphy's

Church's Law dictates that every time you bring a friend to church, it will be the Sunday they preach about money.

There will be parables taught. Eyes of needles mentioned. Foolish rich and rich-poor explained in metaphoric, though sometimes less than poetic, fashion. We will wince when we see the topic announced on the screen up front, uneasy that our friend will think the adage "all churches just want your money" might just be true. We will sit nervously and hope nothing terribly uncomfortable happens.

Churches know that you are sitting anxiously waiting for the moment to pass, wishing you had volunteered to work with kids that morning, and really rethinking your choice to bring a friend. Subsequently, the church is very nervous talking about money. And it has reason to be.

Times Have Changed. Churches are learning to talk about the new realities of the business of running a church. They're engaging the theological aspects of money in an earthly system always striving to figure out what is evil and what is not. And they are moving just as quickly as they can.

In the meantime, we are facing some other fears when it comes to tackling the money monster in the house of God.

Missing The Mark. We are afraid of alienating a certain demographic. Afraid of addressing money to both the rich and poor, as well as the younger crowd affected with colloquially yet accurately described cases of "affluenza". Do we need a different money message for everyone?

We know that God's purpose is to align wealth with His vision. So it doesn't matter whether you are rich or poor or wherever in between – the principles are the same. It is not alienating to say to someone with one talent, "God has a plan for you." It is exciting and hopeful. It isn't insulting to someone with 10 talents to suggest, "You can have a lot of money. It's just a matter of your heart, what you pursue and desire. That is what God cares about."

Poverty Confusion. There has been a misinterpretation of the value of poverty across much of Christendom, and this misrepresentation has given way to a script that essentially robs the wealthy of salvation and treats them as second-class citizens.

When we are unaware of the purpose of something, we have a tendency to abuse it. And by not understanding the purpose of wealth, the Church has had a long history of using poverty to shame the wealthy. This is a misunderstanding and mishandling of God's abundance.

Exposure and Shame. Rich or poor, talking about money exposes what people really care about. When there's a call to action regarding where our treasure is, people do not like their treasure held up to a mirror in front of them.

We are afraid of eliciting guilt. But talking about money by way of guilt is not what we should be doing anyway. God is not a God of shame. The purpose of money and the new mindset that come with it are an opportunity for people to align with God's plan for their own lives. It is a positive thing, not a negative one.

In the same way admitting you have a problem is the first tenet of any 12-step program, the first step to being able to talk about money is to admit that you need to talk about it.

Here's why we need to talk about it.

We Need Help. Most of Christendom has a centuries-long misunderstanding of both the vow of poverty and the purpose of wealth. This widespread, historic misunderstanding of God's purpose for wealth affects the local church today, too.

In a way it seems funny that we are nervous to talk about money. It's one of the most universal topics and one that every single person sitting in a church service on Sunday deals with every single day of their life. They buy and sell and invest and dream and plan with money. Every. Single. Day. So it seems strange that we would be so reticent to talk about something we all have in common.

Not only is money a relatable topic, it's one that we all need some help with. We need to learn God's vision for money. We need practical ways to align with that vision.

The toll that finance takes on the hour-by-hour life of a family is sometimes great and we need to be encouraged that God is using this upheaval, today, for you and for His purpose.

So it's time to slay the dragon. It's time to look money right in the face and say you are not afraid of it.

NO NEED TO BE AFRAID

Henry Ford was a brilliant business mind but his fear got the best of him just like fear can get the best of us.

God offers us a hopeful solution. He wants us to overcome our fear and enjoy the journey. As we journey through this book, I am hopeful that you will become at peace.

Are you tired of trying to outrun your economic fears? Do you feel like you are working too hard? Always anxious and on a treadmill? Good news—Jesus says you can stop running.

"Come to me, all you who are weary and burdened, and I will give you rest" *(Matthew 11:28, NIV)*

"Do not fear" is one of the most repeated commands in the Bible. God links it to His overall plan and to money, over and over and over again. God's plan for wealth is for His purpose, and His purpose is good. He uses it to align money with His vision and He will allow us—you, me, our churches, our businesses—to operate inside of the earthly economy to do so.

Fear is incompatible with God's vision.

Now that we've discussed it, what do we do about it? If fear is one of the biggest concerns addressed in the Bible and a recurring theme Jesus seems to be concerned with, then what does He say? He says this:

"So don't be afraid, little flock. For it gives your Father great happiness to give you the Kingdom." (Luke 12:32, NLT)

And remember how Matthew reminded us to seek first the kingdom of God and His righteousness and that He will provide us everything we need? Well, the verse continues –

"So don't worry about tomorrow." (Matthew 6:34, NLT)

Jesus says not to worry about tomorrow and reminds us hundreds of times to stop worrying about the stuff tomorrow will bring.

Do not worry about food.

Do not worry about clothes.

Do not worry about what others around you think.

"Remember the Kingdom?" He asks. Seek that.

We are safe. Fear Not.

CHAPTER 4

THE GODS OF ECONOMY:
GOD OR MAMMON

*"Money won't make you happy,
but everybody wants to find out for themselves."*
Zig Ziglar

Money makes so many things possible. Money can buy us an education, provide medicine and medical care, and help us build savings for both retirement and rainy days. It can also fund vacations and family togetherness. Money can go to providing for the poor, giving to our communities, and creating housing programs for refugees. Not to mention that since most of us don't grow our own food, make our own clothes, or build our own houses, we also need money for even our most basic needs.

We need money. And whether we are exchanging it for a pizza, a movie, or we are signing away millions for a dream piece of real estate, we exchange it for worthwhile things all the time. Daily, in fact. Sometimes hourly.

So you'd think we would be comfortable with how money intersects with our regular life, but the truth is we are anything but.

The Problem With The Paycheck

More than half of Canadian and American households live paycheck to paycheck and the amount of debt in those households continues to grow. People are stressing out about how to meet their own needs, and they're doing so every 30 days.

But money stress is about more than just the money itself. It's more than looking at the sum of our bank accounts. It's about how we interact with money.

We are always thinking about it. We are continually pursuing it, trusting that it will do its job: provide for our needs, our wants, and everything in our life. That's a lot of mental and emotional real estate for something that has been widely proven not to make us happy or satisfied.[1]

We act as though money is directly connected to fulfillment in our job, but it's not true. There is a very thin connection between salary and happiness with our jobs. At a high income, you aren't more likely to be satisfied with your job than someone at a lower income. Plus, both poverty and wealth each has their inherent issues. Money can make people paranoid and anxious and it can cloud your moral judgment. So rich or poor, the money itself isn't the issue. We make it, we spend it, we worry about it, and we try to find power in it.

Our culture has worked hard to make us discontent, and guess what? They've won for the most part. Society wants us to think there is never enough and we should bind ourselves to the cycle of looking for meaning in making more money.

Regardless, I have good news for you. There is hope. There is a perfect economic system designed and guaranteed to prosper you into your future and I am going to explain how to participate in it.

Before we can participate, though, we must first understand the two different economic structures vying for your attention and also the gods who govern them. One will continue to stress you

---

[1] Butler, J. (2017). Can money make you happy? Financial Times LTD. Retrieved from: https://www.ft.com/content/208627f2-d1d0-11e6-9341-7393bb2e1b51

out, steal your joy, and eventually bankrupt you at some level. The other will give you hope, bring you peace, and prosper you into your future.

WE HAVE TWO CHOICES: GOD OR MAMMON

"No servant can serve two masters; for either he will hate the one and love the other, or else he will be loyal to the one and despise the other. You cannot serve God and mammon." (Luke 16:13, NKJV)

The word mammon finds its roots in the Chaldeans of Babylon from the region of ancient Mesopotamia, a culture very sensitive to the spirit realm that was rooted in idol worship and was very demon-centric. Mammon means wealth personified. It means three things: physical money, the system that uses money to enslave, and the spirit attached to money. Mammon is the god over the economy of this world. Mammon is a personality, a spirit seeking to express itself through money and enslave people. Let me put it another way: Satan is the god of this world and Mammon is the CFO.[2]

No wonder Jesus draws a clear and distinct line between serving money and serving God. Nowhere else in the Bible is there a more direct contrast between God and any other personality. It's important to note that it is possible to be a recipient of salvation and yet live out your life in enslavement to money. This could be the case whether you are rich or poor, needy or greedy, and loving or hating money. If you serve Mammon you will be a slave to money, but if you serve God, money will serve you.

In the entire Bible, no one talks about Mammon except for Jesus, even though Mammon's economy has been functioning in this world since the fall of Adam in the Garden of Eden. Why does Jesus address it? Because Jesus is the Lord of Heaven's Armies

---

2 2 Corinthians 4:4

and as such is the CFO over God's economy—the economy of the Kingdom. This economy is far superior to the economy of this world. It works **in** the everyday economy of the world but it is not **of** it.

First, God owns the earth, the cattle, the silver and gold and all the people that dwell in it.[3] From an economic viewpoint that means all the real estate, intellectual property, precious metals, and mineral rights belong to Him. He is also the Land Lord and we are the lessees of the planet entrusted to steward it. However, even though all the wealth belongs to God, not all of it is under His management.

Mind you, today money does not have any intrinsic value, as it no longer backed by gold. But it still has a strong connection with the spirit world. That's why Jesus said those that trust in riches would find it very difficult to enter the Kingdom of God[4] To trust in riches is to trust in Satan (Mammon)—the god of this world. Before you jump ship and go off on some religious trail let me keep your focus on God's intention here. Your heart is the most precious currency in the Kingdom of God and it should be guarded with all diligence for out of it flow all the streams of life.[5]

Any time you get serious about serving God with all your heart and advancing His Kingdom, you will be faced with the decision to choose between Mammon and God. Your loyalties will be tested whether you are wealthy, middle class, or are literally poor. Prior to this juncture in your life you would have been living unaware of the governance of Mammon over your life. But now God is getting ready to entrust you with more important things like the true riches of His Kingdom. (We'll explain "true riches" in a bit.)

This does not mean God wants you to make a vow of poverty and give away all you have, as religious people would have you

---

3 Psalm 24:1, Haggai 2:8
4 Mark 10:24-2,
5 Proverbs 4:23

believe. However, Jesus did ask a rich young ruler to sell all that he had and give it all away to follow him. The young ruler turned down the offer because his heart trusted in money and so he chose to serve Mammon instead. As a result, he missed out on an opportunity of a lifetime. It was in this context Jesus made the statement that anyone who gives up wealth to follow Him would receive a 100-fold return here on earth and in eternity to come.[6] Jesus added "with persecution"—courtesy of the religious people.

UNRIGHTEOUS MAMMON

Jesus makes another interesting statement about Mammon.

"Therefore if you have not been faithful in the UNRIGHTEOUS MAMMON, who will commit to your trust the true riches?"[7] (Luke 16:11, NKJV)

Notice the word unrighteous as the description of money in the above text. Here Jesus is referring to the spirit attached to money and worldly wealth when detached from God's economy. A dysfunctional religious mind set would take this out of context and claim that since money is evil, by default wealthy people are also evil and therefore they cannot be spiritual. Or, worse, that poverty is the way to obtain a mansion in heaven. Meanwhile Jesus is saying the exact opposite, that if you handle money properly, you are more spiritual and therefore will be entrusted with the true riches—beyond this world—that are heavenly and eternal in value. So what does this mean? It means by default money has the spirit of Mammon attached to it.

God wants you to handle money and steward it well but this does not only mean good management of money in general. We often confuse God's definition of stewardship with good money management and although that is part of it, it is not the full meaning here. I am sure you know people who manage money well and make

---
6   Mark 10:30
7   Emphasis added

good investments but are not necessarily spiritual. True stewardship is about bringing money out of Mammon's control and placing under God's management. He is the true owner of it all and He entrusts us with the grace of such stewardship. God wants you to steward what He already has title to!

We do this by investing it in the gospel to advance His Kingdom and build the House of God. In doing so we move money out of this world and invest it in our heavenly accounts.[8] This has profound natural and spiritual implications. First, God multiplies the impact of our seed capital for use in His vision and we receive a favorable return on our investment. Second, the money we now have is no longer attached to the spirit of Mammon and is uniquely blessed in its use. In other words, it is clean and no longer unrighteous but holy with God's Spirit on it. This process is basically reverse money laundering. This is what Jesus meant when he admonished us not to invest our treasure in this volatile world but to lay it up in heaven.[9] He was referring to this process of taking money out of Mammon's economy and investing it in God's economy. Your role in this process is true stewardship of His assets.

When sin entered the world, through the fall of Adam, it corrupted everything and that's when the wealth of the world became Mammon and came under the governance of Satan—the god of this world.[10] Since then, the whole earth, including the gold, silver, and all the wealth of the world with the rest of creation is yearning to be redeemed like God's children.[11] That's why money is crying out to the Lord of Heaven's Armies, and reporting on its abusers and asking to be reassigned to Gods original intent.[12]

Let's take another look at Abel who gave God the firstborn and absolute best from his flock and found acceptance. Through this offering the spirit of Mammon attached to his money and

---

8 Matthew 6:20
9 Matthew 6:19-20
10 2 Corinthians 4:4
11 Romans 8:20-22
12 James 5:4

livelihood was removed and the rest of his business came under the governance of God's Spirit. The blessing was now attached to his money and it would continue to align the spirit realm with the movement of his money. His unrighteous Mammon got redeemed out of one economy into another. His gift had a tangible impact in the spirit realm and that is why his offering still speaks today.[13] He was faithful with unrighteous Mammon and was certainly entrusted with true riches.

Cain, on the other hand, did not give God the first fruits of his crops. His entire business was functioning under the spirit of Mammon. The rest of his story did not go well.

Remember, God intends for you to learn how to manage and steward the wealth of the world to help accomplish His vision. God's economic system takes money out of the control of those who serve Mammon and transfers it into the hands of those who trust God and are stewards in God's economy.

In light of the above lets understand how this process works.

GOD'S ECONOMY: SEED TIME AND HARVEST

"As long as the earth endures, seedtime and harvest...will never cease." (Genesis 8:22, NIV)

Notice after the grand big flush in Noah's day, God promised to never destroy the earth and He reinstituted the law of seedtime and harvest. This law is not only natural but also spiritual. It extends beyond God's economy and it is universal to the Kingdom of God.

God's economy is a generational economy that works, in many ways, like a regular investment system. There's investing, compound interest, and generational wealth. It is a sowing and

---

13 Hebrew 11:4, Genesis 4:4

reaping economy, which means what we plant and invest today will be harvested into the future. God calls this seedtime and harvest. We sow in one season and reap in another.

The big difference is that we aren't the ones who provide the seed capital. God provides the seed. The seed is supplied by God and sown by us. It's an investment. It's capital for your future. Wherever it is sown it multiplies both in impact and return. In addition to the seed, God also supplies bread in this system. Bread is everything you need in life: food, shelter, clothes, education for your kids, vehicles and homes, etc. Everything you need for your family to live on this earth in abundance is covered in the category of bread. Not everyone starts with the same amount of seed or bread, but the principle for how you manage each is the same: God will continually supply both to you, so sow your seed and eat your bread in confidence knowing and trusting that God will continue to provide. Just remember never to eat your seed or sow your bread. This is the wrong system, and if you do this you will eat your seed all your life and you will never have any to sow into your future.

They refer to generosity as waste and scarcity as prudence.

By contrast, the world's economy is a "buy and sell" economy. It inhabits the mind set of leverage and trade. Money is the currency of leverage, fluctuating all the time, and we exchange it for what we value. The world's economy is based on a debt-based system designed to enslave most at the benefit of a few. Remember, money today has no intrinsic value since it is no longer secured by gold—but that is another story.

God's economy is not about leverage at all. It's all about sowing out of the world's system into God's system. And it's about reaping from God's economy, both in this world and in the world to come. We will look at practical ways and how this works in chapter 6.

GOD TOUCH MY HEART BUT NOT MY WALLET

There is one other pseudo-economy and it is a dysfunctional religious hybrid of the world's economy and God's economy. It's just another face of Mammon but with God's name attached to it. I have pointed out this way of thinking a few times already throughout the book. This mindset embraces poverty but secretly pursues money. It pretends not to care about money but deeply loves it. It considers wealthy people generally evil and themselves pious for thinking that way. The mention of money in a church setting offends religious people but they think about it all the time. They refer to generosity as waste and scarcity as prudence. Religious people want God to touch their heart but not their money. Remember, Jesus made it clear that the root of the religious spirit is the love of money.[14]

Let's go back to the Gospel of Matthew for a minute.

"Your eye is like a lamp that provides light for your body. When your eye is healthy, your whole body is filled with light. But when your eye is unhealthy, your whole body is filled with darkness. And if the light you think you have is actually darkness, how deep that darkness is!" (Matthew 6:22-23, NLT)

If the desire of your eye is treasure and money, this will lead to darkness. But if your eye desires Him, to establish His Covenant and His Kingdom, then your life will be full of light. In other words, you can't have a dual vision. You can only have eyes for one thing – one desire. It can't be to establish His Covenant and something else.

So if you can only have one desire and that one desire is to align

---

14 Luke 16:14

with God's vision, that means something important:

Your needs cannot be your desire.

"No one can serve two masters; for either he will hate the one and love the other, or else he will be loyal to the one and despise the other. You cannot serve God and mammon." (Matthew 6:24, NKJV)

Once again we see how desire for money and treasure, whether it's for our needs or something else, falls under Mammon's system.

BIG LIE ENDS IN A BAD DAY: ANANIAS & SAPPHIRA

For context, I would like to share a story about a New Testament couple who chose to function in this dysfunctional religious hybrid economy. The apostles had recently experienced persecution from the religious leaders for performing a notable miracle confirming the message of Christ. The Holy Spirit in turn empowered them to preach the message with even more boldness.[15]

And with great power the apostles gave witness to the resurrection of the Lord Jesus. And great grace was upon them all. Nor was there anyone among them who lacked; for all who were possessors of lands or houses sold them, and brought the proceeds of the things that were sold, and laid them at the apostles' feet; and they distributed to each as anyone had need. (Acts 4:33-35, NKJV)

During this pivotal time, God's economy was functioning in the early church and the people understood God was their provider. People were selling homes and land, laying the proceeds at the feet of the Apostles. Fields were big deals in that day; real estate, as it is now, was all the rage. The economy of sowing and reaping

---

15 Acts 4:31

was in motion and there was plenty of supply for everyone and the work of the Apostles' ministry. However, Mammon was looking for a way in.

Meet Ananias & Sapphira: a reputable wealthy couple known amongst the people. They were operating in Mammon's economy, though my guess is they'd convinced themselves they were doing otherwise. This is one of the hallmarks of this dysfunctional religious mindset: it tricks you into thinking you're operating in God's economy while you are trusting in Mammon. They gave the impression they were giving 100% of the proceeds like others, but meanwhile they were keeping back a portion of the proceeds for themselves. Now they did not have to give it at all, but to lie about their giving for the sake of recognition and notoriety reveals they had a motive. And their pursuit ended with them buried under the land instead of living on top of it.

Ananias and Sapphira did what we sometimes do. They held back the seed God provided for them to sow. Instead of bringing all of it to the Apostles, they kept some of the money to provide for themselves. Maybe their motive was elicited by some well-meaning leader who encouraged them to sell their field and keep the profits because that would a responsible way to handle God's money. Either way they were trusting in money.

Enter: Mammon's economy (that was fast, wasn't it?).

The primary reason they kept part of the proceeds was this: they were operating from within a buy-sell mindset. They intended to leverage the money they were giving to gain recognition and so they schemed to lie about the amount. Giving with strings attached is not really giving. Our motivation for giving is as important as giving. Generosity and giving are the result of genuine love. They had the freedom to sell or keep their field and the profits were theirs to give away as they chose. However, instead of sowing the land as promised purely for purpose of the Kingdom and then reaping the ensuing multiplication, they tried to use giving as a means to buy notoriety and respect. They trusted money instead of God and loved money more than God. When they brought the proceeds to the church, they lied and told the apostles it was the full amount.

They jumped into the wrong economy and then lied about it. They trusted in money and what it could buy them. They thought they could buy something that sowing could not: approval and acceptance. And since our hearts always follow our treasure,[16] money exposed their hearts in the form of a lie. Things went quickly downhill.

"Peter said, 'Ananias, why have you let Satan fill your heart? You lied to the Holy Spirit, and you kept some of the money for yourself. The property was yours to sell or not sell, as you wished. And after selling it, the money was also yours to give away. How could you do a thing like this? You weren't lying to us but to God!'" (Acts 5:3-4, NLT)

And then Ananias dropped dead. Just fell right there on the floor at the sound of Peter's words and was gone. Understandably everyone around him was immediately afraid. After a while some younger men went about the business of wrapping and burying the guy.

Sapphira's day didn't end much better.

About three hours after Ananias' death, Sapphira, still unaware of her husband's untimely demise, wandered in to find Peter, who had a few questions about the whole field thing. "Was this the price you and your husband received for your land?" Peter asked. "Yes," she replied, "that was the price."

"And Peter said, 'How could the two of you even think of conspiring to test the Spirit of the Lord like this? The young men who buried your husband are just outside the door, and they will carry you out, too." (v. 9)

---

16 Matthew 6:21

And just like that and as promised, Sapphira fell to the floor and was dead. The young men who'd drawn the short grave-digging straws grabbed another sheet, knocked the dirt off their shovels and went about burying her, too. An even greater reverent honor and fear settled into the entire church.

Nevertheless, because of the Apostles' ministry even greater numbers of believers were being added to the church.

But no one else dared to join them, even though all the people had high regard for them. Yet more and more people believed and were brought to the Lord – crowds of both men and women. As a result of the apostles' work, sick people were brought out into the streets on beds and mats so that Peter's shadow might fall across some of them as he went by. Crowds came from the villages around Jerusalem, bringing their sick and those possessed by evil spirits, and they were all healed. (Acts 5:13-16, NLT)

This was the purpose of money in the Church. The seed capital being sown into the Apostles' ministry was multiplying into more and more believers. People were being healed. Evil spirits were being dispossessed. The dead were being raised back to life.

Since God is the source of life then the opposite must also be true. Sin is the source of death. God doesn't promise to kill people in the New Testament Church. God tries to protect them from the consequences of their sin—but if they just don't want that protection eventually He leaves them to their own self-destructive end.[17] By trying to impress the apostles and the church with money, Ananias had let Satan and Satan's economy fill his heart. Apparently evil just eventually played itself out.

By lying to man, Ananias and Sapphira were lying to God. Have you ever told a lie even though there was no reason to? Have you ever had a child or a co-worker do so? Those lies are dually puzzling. Like those, this one was juvenile and senseless – they

---

17 Romans 1:24-26

already had the land and could use it even after it was sold. They didn't stand to gain anything by it and, had they lived, it also would have cost them their credibility. This is short-sighted thinking. It is what happens when you don't align with God's vision. It's also what happens when you trust an economy that isn't ever going to give you what you want and need.

So there was a lack of trust in God's plan. They were loyal to Mammon rather than to God. You cannot serve God and Mammon. Ananias and Sapphira were operating within a buy-sell financial system instead of a sowing and reaping one. They desired money, trusting it and what it could do for them instead of trusting God and His economy. They desired to meet their own needs and they pursued the approval of others rather than seeking God first. They were trying to measure success within a system that was taking them in circles.

Mammon in the world's economy seduces your desire, enlists your trust and competes for your pursuit.

We are sometimes tempted to do the same thing. But God has a different plan and the return on the investment in His economy is guaranteed.

God's economy provides for our needs and gives us hope and significance. When we desire God, we have hope. When we trust God to meet our needs, He does. When we pursue God, we find our significance. It's a perfect system.

Before we can talk further about how to operate within God's economy, we need to discuss the characteristics of Mammon's economy and how it differs from God's. We will also discuss how the two compete for our allegiance and what we can do to ensure that we are participating in a system that will work forever.

DESIRING, TRUSTING, AND PURSUING MONEY

Mammon in the world's economy seduces your desire, enlists your trust, and competes for your pursuit. The world desires treasure and money and seeks after it.

"'I will shake all the nations; and they will come with the wealth of all nations, and I will fill this house with glory,' says the LORD of hosts." (Haggai 2:7, NASB)

Here is another translation that makes it even clearer.

"'I will shake all nations, and what is DESIRED by all nations will come, and I will fill this house with glory,' says the LORD Almighty" (Haggai 2:7, NIV)

The world desires wealth and Jesus, in reference to our material needs, confirmed it this way.

"For all these things the nations of the world seek after, and your Father knows that you need these things. (Luke 12:30, NKJV)

Your Heavenly Father cares for you and your physical and material needs. He has a process for those needs to be met as we seek Him, seek His Kingdom, and build His House.

THE PROBLEM IN OUR PRAYER

Anytime we trust, desire, and pursue something important, it can become a competing god. Money is no different. The need for money or the worry over it can consume our time and energy so completely that it becomes the thing we think about, obsess over, and can't get enough of. It becomes an addiction. Addiction is...well, we know what addiction is.

You may not believe that you desire, trust, and pursue money. You certainly may not believe that you are addicted to it. But consider this: you may have gotten off course in the place you least expected it to happen.

It may have started out in prayer.

How could praying, of all things, send us away from seeking God and instead send us off in hot pursuit of money? We are more susceptible to this happening than you may think.

First, one of the things we ask for in prayer is for God to meet our needs. This is good and a prayer that is prayed all the time. God has promised to provide our needs, right? Isn't this what we are supposed to be praying?

Yes, but what happens is; when we pray for our needs to be met, often the answer to that prayer comes in the form of financial supply. You may get a new job, or a promotion or your business grows and you get busy about life, forgetting God granted you the means of that provision in the first place. At the same time you are being bombarded with messages from the world to desire and trust in money and you are constantly reminded of the fear of losing it. Remember, the primary purpose of money is not to meet our needs and we have to be deliberate to put God and His vision first in our finances. Otherwise, subtle shifts take place in our heart, creating a dependence on money.

We have learned stewardship extends beyond the scope of natural management of money to participating in His economy. Without that understanding we end up desiring God to supply money to us so that we can meet our own needs and be about our business. It is easy to forget God supplied the money and instead focus on what money does for us. Once again money, detached from its purpose, starts to move our heart in the wrong direction. Our process on very basic level can start to look like this:

PRAY ⇨ MAKE ENOUGH MONEY ⇨ MEET OUR OWN NEEDS

God didn't say "consider the lilies of the field and the birds of the sky" because they know how to manage money and they are capable of meeting their own needs with it.[18] No. God says, "I will meet your needs." Period. He doesn't say He is necessarily even going to do it with money. He meets our needs in many ways. Otherwise we are making Him subject to the limitations of the world. As it is in heaven so let it be on earth.

Without the right foundation in prayer we can begin desiring money and trusting it to meet our needs. We may think we are trusting in God but in reality we are trusting in money. And then a course of action is set in place—we begin pursuing money. Right away our sense of desire and trust becomes about money—sometimes ironically while we are still praying.

It looks and sounds like God's economy, but it's just another symptom of the dysfunctional religious hybrid of God's and Mammon's economy.

The Problem of Priorities

The key to God's economy is that we desire, trust, and pursue *Him*, not money. And yet we can be trapped quite easily in trusting money, even in prayer. What are we supposed to do, then?

The Gospel of Matthew says this:

"But seek first his kingdom and his righteousness, and all these things will be given to you as well." (Matthew 6:33, NIV)

How does seeking God first provide anything for us?

This seems upside down. Seek God first; and then all of these things will be given. It doesn't say seek to provide for yourself and God will repay your responsibility. It doesn't say that we need to worry about how our children are going to eat and that God will

---

18 Matthew 6:27-28

reward us for fastidious attention to detail. We sometimes learn as much from what the text doesn't say as what it does.

Seek first—This verse is all about focus, about priorities, and about our desire for God and His Kingdom. Maybe your motivation for money is noble. Maybe you had parents who didn't provide for you and you don't want to repeat the cycle with your family. So you trust money. You trust you.

Sometimes we look to the same systems that have harmed us and ask for them to fix us.

Trusting yourself means you are responsible for your wealth, for meeting your own needs. It also makes money responsible for several other very important things: your identity, your happiness, and your power. It leaves you in control.

Trusting in God means that God will provide for you and for your family. It means your identity is secure in Christ, your joy is in the Kingdom and God gives you the power to get wealth to participate in His vision. When you're seeking Mammon you just want more – whether you have little or much. When you're seeking God, you want more of God and you always have everything you need.

Though we will delve into these in much more detail, consider this quick view of some of these differences between Mammon's economy and God's:

	Mammon's Economy	God's Economy
We Love	Money	God
We Trust	Money	God
Time Spent	Pursuing money	Pursuing God
Vision	Temporary	Eternal
Focus	Me	God
Talent	Earned or inherited	Given by God
Money Anxiety	Necessary	Unnecessary
Financial Freedom	At risk	Guaranteed

The apostle Paul's first letter to Timothy says it this way:

"Teach those who are rich in this world not to be proud and not to trust in their money, which is so unreliable. Their trust should be in God, who richly gives us all we need for our enjoyment." (I Timothy 6:17, NLT)

What do you enjoy? Golf? Shopping? Enjoy it. Just don't trust in it. Have it, but don't desire it. Desire God. In other words, it's ok to have a nice car as long as the car doesn't have you. Anything that has you rules over you.

We know that Mammon's economy will eventually make money rule over us. But none of us sets out with the goal of being held captive by it. We certainly don't set out to stay imprisoned forever. But we're likely in chains without even knowing it.

Going In Circles: Worrying About Tomorrow

God created us to be talented, creative, intelligent people. This doesn't have to be secondary to providing for us, because we aren't meant to be meeting our own needs anyway.

"Desire Me," God says. "Trust Me," He reminds us. "Pursue Me and you will have everything you need."

This is easier than it sounds. We continue to circle the frenetic pit of providing for us. Some may even choose to hold vigil there. Why?

Because we often equate most of our needs with money.

We never get a break from our needs. We never wake up and think, "I don't have a single need today. If I eat, fine. If not, that's fine, too. If I don't have a roof over my kid's head, no biggie. And if I wear out all of my clothes or if my kid grows out of hers, that's no problem. Nudity is perfectly acceptable." Obviously not. It doesn't work that way. We are constantly looking for ways to meet today's needs while at the same time worrying about tomorrow's and the day after that and the day after that.

Worry is a condition of an inherently broken system. There's no end in sight. There's no solution. Worry is never part of the solution and worrying about money and our needs is like running in circles.

A flawed economy can be exhausting. We often desire for money to meet our physical and emotional needs. As a result, we earn more, buy more, and then spend and borrow more to house all of the things we've bought. In our search for security and joy we are happy for about 30 seconds. But Jesus reminds us:

"Therefore I say to you, do not worry about your life, what you will eat or what you will drink; nor about your body, what you will put on. Is not life more than food and the body more than clothing?" (Matthew 6:25, NKJV)

In other words, God is asking us, "Do you think this is the only reason I put you in this world is to figure out what to wear or how to eat or survive?"

And the answer is No. Matthew continues with this peaceful

reminder—

Consider the Birds and the Lilies

"Look at the birds of the air, for they neither sow nor reap nor gather into barns; yet your heavenly Father feeds them. Are you not of more value than they?" (v 26)

They are provided for without doing anything. They work, sure, but they don't worry about tomorrow. You are way more important than birds.

Can all your worries add a single moment to your life?

"So why do you worry about clothing? Consider the lilies of the field, how they grow: they neither toil nor spin; and yet I say to you that even Solomon in all his glory was not arrayed like one of these" (v 28-29)

Solomon was the wealthiest guy around and it's likely his clothing was the best there was. In fact, we are going to talk a lot about him again in Chapter 7. His whole household, including his servants, were dressed more elaborately than anyone.

"And if God cares so wonderfully for wildflowers that are here today and thrown in to the fire tomorrow, he will certainly care for you. Why do you have so little faith?

So don't worry about these things, saying, 'What will we eat? What will we drink? What will we wear?' These things dominate the thoughts of unbelievers, but your heavenly Father already knows all your needs. (v 30-32, NLT)

And we come back to the instructive part:

"Seek the Kingdom of God above all else, and live righteously, and he will give you everything you need." (v 33)

God knows we have physical needs. Even the birds of the air and lilies of the field do. But our physical needs are met by seeking Him. Period.

One last note about this passage. The image of the bird is particularly evocative here because the picture of a bird in flight is commonly associated with freedom.

Realizing we already have everything we need is what finally sets us free.

Good News For The Economy: God Will Provide

Even though we are not part of the first-century Church and cannot call any of the Apostles and invite them to dinner, it's still likely that we recognize ourselves in Ananias and Sapphira's story. Do you ever trust in the wrong system? Are you thinking that the pursuit of notoriety and influence is the way to provide for yourself? Has buy-sell economics crept into what God is asking of you?

You have no cash value. I don't have any cash value, either. I would not trade my wife for a new car or a nice vacation. I wouldn't trade her for the best piece of real estate either because none of us would ever trade away what's most important in our lives. God created them. And there is no amount of cash that would be worth trading them away.

Economics Unbound: Living Free

Mammon's economy holds us captive in a circle of self-provision. God's economy offers a get out of jail free card.

Financial freedom means that by desiring and trusting in God rather than in money, I can:

- Allow wealth to be a tool God uses, not a tool I trust to meet my own needs. God will use money to align the world's resources with His vision. And we are a part of that. But meeting our own daily needs – that's God's job, not ours. We get to concentrate on the larger story God is writing about the world.

- Find my self-worth based on who I am in Christ. It means I can be content in who I was created to be. I get to concentrate on the story God is writing about me.

- Choose my career and my work/life balance according to my convictions and giftedness, not according to what will meet my needs first. It means I have the time to pursue excellence and artistic and creative giftedness without the pressure of performing just for others. The work can be for the work itself.

- Pursue what I feel called to do without worrying about failure. It allows me to be a respecter of deadlines and goals without feeling pressured by them.

- Avoid buying and selling in hopes of fame and notoriety and the approval of anyone else.

CEASE STRIVING: GOOD NEWS FOR FREE PEOPLE

It's God's job to meet our needs and it's our job to seek Him. Because of this, we can move from a take-charge mentality to one of surrender and freedom.

The Psalmist says this:

"Cease striving and know that I am God" (Psalm 46:10, NASB).

Cease striving. Stop pursuing, trusting and spending your valuable time desiring money. Buy and sell things, fine. But responsibly participate in God's economy, sowing your seed and eating your bread, and stewarding well what has been given to you. Operate inside the world's economy, not of it, knowing that God will provide for your needs. And believe that everything is a gift from God. This will bring gratitude.

Paul's letter to Timothy reminds us that ceasing striving leaves room for something else: peace.

"But godliness actually is a means of great gain when accompanied by contentment." (1 Timothy 6:6, NASB)

Godliness brings about true financial peace. In fact, if your eyes are on establishing God's vision, you don't have a desire for money at all. This is not to say that you will not be wealthy, but it does indicate a complete change of mindset. You seek first the Kingdom. And the King of the Kingdom, and His domain of influence. And that's all you're focused on.

WEALTH AND GOD'S HOUSE: BUILDING A SPIRITUAL HABITATION

In his letter to the church at Ephesus, Paul gives us insight into something else that is, once again, spiritual and physical at the same time. As a part of God's vision, we are asked to build a spiritual habitation. He describes this idea of the house of God and he says this:

"So now you Gentiles are no longer strangers and foreigners. You are citizens along with all of God's holy people. You are members of God's family.

Together, we are his house, built on the foundation of the apostles and the prophets. And the cornerstone is Christ Jesus himself. We are carefully joined together in him, becoming a holy temple for the Lord. Through him you Gentiles are also being made part of this dwelling where God lives by his Spirit." (Ephesians 2:19-22, NLT)

The House of God has a through line beginning with the prophets and Apostles and continuing to this day. This house, it turns out, is really important.

Haggai and The Temple of Doom

Haggai was an Old Testament prophet who was dealing with an age-old problem.

God's people were greedy.

Everywhere He looked they were lining their walls with fancy wood paneling. This doesn't seem entirely dramatic to us – we can walk into any home improvement store and panel our walls in just about anything we desire and at any price we want. However in those days this was a luxury. Stone was cheap but wood...wood was expensive. And the people needed their homes to look expensive.

The people wore clothing and, because they were never satisfied with what was in their closets, they kept buying more. As a result they needed to build bigger closets. Then they went to "Promised Land Costco: and bought large quantities of food. So they built bigger pantries. They were unsatisfied with their jobs and equally as unsatisfied with the possessions they acquired with their paychecks. The more they spent, the more this was true and they never seemed to have enough.

So God asked Haggai to get the people's attention.

"Look at what's happening to you! You have planted much but harvest little. You eat but are not satisfied. You drink but are still thirsty. You put on clothes but cannot keep warm. Your wages disappear as though you were putting them in pockets filled with holes!" (Haggai 1:5-6, NLT)

Does that sounds familiar?

Meanwhile...God's house was a mess.[19]

The temple was in ruins and God's people seemed to have their

---

19 Haggai 1:4

own word from God, the kind of word that conveniently lined up letter by letter with exactly what they did and didn't want to do: "The time has not yet come to rebuild the house of the Lord," they said. Funny that it wasn't time to rebuild God's house but it certainly seemed time to build their own. They were keeping up with the Joneses big time.

God often lets irony have its day. Despite their perceived standard of living, the people were basically...broke. They were in an economic slump. There was a drought on their land and the land dried up, the harvests were poor, and their livestock were starving.

God sent a message to Haggai that he needed to remind the people that not only are there shakings to produce alignment and battles to get control back over the economy, but that their hearts would follow where their money went. They needed to get out of their own houses and back into God's, to get their minds off serving themselves and back into God's vision. "Get your money back to the right priorities and your heart will follow it", God says. "And I will be there".[20]

God tells them to get busy rebuilding the temple. "You can do it," God tells them. "I am with you. You're struggling because you've put yourself and not My house first." God's House is integral to His vision and His economy.

As the people began to align their finances and put Gods House first, God immediately blessed them and their economy. It's amazing how as a result God prospered the economy of the whole nation. See, putting money in its right place aligns the spirit realm over us.

Later God spoke to the people again through Haggai, giving them further insight into His plan about wealth and His House:

"For this is what the Lord of Heaven's Armies says: In just a

---

20 Matthew 6:21

little while I will again shake the heavens and the earth, the oceans and the dry land. I will shake all the nations, and the treasures of all the nations will be brought to this Temple. I will fill this place with glory, says the Lord of Heaven's Armies. The silver is mine, and the gold is mine, says the Lord of Heaven's Armies. The future glory of this Temple will be greater than its past glory, says the Lord of Heaven's Armies. And in this place I will bring peace." (Haggai 2:6-9, NLT)

God reminds them and us that all the silver, gold, and wealth of the world actually belong to Him. How does God shake a nation? He shakes its economy to re-align wealth with His purpose and channel it into the House of God. Notice wealth has a destination and that destination is God's house. The House of God is the treasury of the Kingdom. It's the Fort Knox of God's economy. It's the main banking hub and it's central to God's purpose for wealth to establish the Abrahamic Covenant and fulfill His vision.

How does wealth get into God's house? It gets into God's house through **you**. God gives **you** the power to create and get wealth in the real world and you bring it to God's House. He prospers your business, increases your real estate, causes your ideas to thrive, multiplies your investments, and releases your inheritance. However, never forget all this wealth belongs to God and you are a steward of His resources. You in turn bring it into His House and redeem the wealth of the world out of Mammon's economy and into His. Your heart follows your money. We need to develop a bigger vision for money. It's not about how much you can hold in your hand but about participating in redeeming all the wealth of the world and placing it in His hands for His vision. This is what God means when he says, "I will shake all nations and bring the wealth and treasure that the world desires into His House."[21] Not only is He going to bring the wealth into His House, He will also bring His Glory and draw the people of the nations, too. When money comes into God's house it is cleansed and becomes available to accomplish God's vision to reach the world.

---

21 Haggai 2:7

Another thing to note here is this term: The Lord of Heaven's Armies.

This sounds ominous and kind of like a tribe of gladiators should be marching in to conquer like in a Hollywood blockbuster. But other translations of this term use the words "Lord of Angel Armies." In other words, God is using an army—a large number—of invisible helpers to protect and guide us, and also to protect and guide the flow of money. There is a war over wealth and Satan is working overtime to keep the minds of people focused on money rather than its purpose.

Let's look at this signature verse out of Deuteronomy again:

"But remember the Lord your God, for it is he who gives you the ability to produce wealth, and so confirms his covenant, which he swore to your ancestors, as it is today." (Deuteronomy 8:18, NIV)

Wealth is not only the means to establish and fulfill the Abrahamic Covenant but also a confirmation of the Covenant. The Hebrew brings more meaning to the words "ability" and "wealth" in the above text. It means that God uses the power of an army and strategy to get wealth. The Lord of Heaven's Armies is at work and He is over God's economy and also over His House.

Haggai asks us to look at our priorities. We've established that it's unsatisfying to keep working and working and spending and spending and saving and saving and never feeling full or warm enough. Haggai's words brought hope both to his people and also to us in the future. God's Spirit was dwelling among them and He has promised peace. He promises the same to us.

We've talked about Mammon's economy and its flawed systems and processes. We've considered the warning signs that we might be operating in it. We've also remembered the birds and the lilies and the God who made them. They are a reminder that He has given us a perfect economy to operate within.

Now, in this more expanded, side-by-side comparison, we can easily consider the vast difference between the two:

	Mammon's Economy	God's Economy
Who owns money?	Ownership is divided between people and government	God owns everything
Who provides money?	We provide for ourselves through work and financial independence	God
Type of Economy	Buy and Sell / Credit and Debit	Sowing and reaping
Resources	Resources are limited and in some cases scarce or depleted	Unlimited: more resources than we can see both in the spiritual and natural realm
Is there inflation?	Yes. Even if it's low, there's eventually always inflation	No, because God supplies all of our needs no matter the cost
Return on Investment	Even 100% return is rare	10,000% (100-fold) guaranteed to all investors
Risk	High	No risk. Everything is guaranteed
Supply and Demand	Supply is limited and includes some amount of a delay	All needs are supplied on time and are unlimited
Treasure	Treasure is stored on earth where it can rot and be stolen	Treasure is stored safely in heaven
Worry	Endless	None
System	Flawed	Perfect
Motivation	Greed	Generosity
Process	Circular	Linear
Goals	Short-term	Eternal
Desire Brings	Anxiety	Hope
Trust	Never trustworthy	Meets our needs
Pursuit ends in	Striving	Significance
Love	Money	God

Pocket Change: Baskets Full of Bread and Hands Full of Seed

When we desire, trust, and pursue money we are willing to sacrifice just about anything—our health, our relationships, and our emotional well-being—to get it. We live with constant anxiety that someone is going to appear at our door and tell us the gig is up, that we are about to be devoured by...by who? We never really know. Eventually our heavy pursuit of money turns on us and we feel like we are being chased by it.

Financial freedom, on the other hand, means we pray for God to provide our needs. We do not pray that He is going to provide money for us to meet our own needs. It means we do not have to keep looking over our shoulder expecting a shortfall to overtake us. It means we trust God and not what's in our bank account—large or small. It means we pursue Him.

Trust that God will function in His economy. Give to every good and charitable work and in doing so you will be free. In reference to the rich:

"Tell them to use their money to do good. They should be rich in good works and generous to those in need, always being ready to share with others. 19 By doing this they will be storing up their treasure as a good foundation for the future so that they may experience true life." (1 Timothy 6:18-19, NLT)

Instead of trusting in money, instead of setting our hope on the uncertainty of riches, we set our hopes in God, who richly provides us with everything to enjoy.

Enjoy?

Yes, enjoy.

Enjoy your tacos, your two months of Netflix, or whatever your endless options. The truth is, it's not money that makes things possible. God is providing your daily bread by way of both your everyday needs and the desires of your heart. Yes, our world spins around money. We can't avoid it, but it is God we need, not money. He alone is the Provider, the Commander of economy, and He moves money for you to steward as tithe, seed, and bread.

Trust God. Pursue God. Desire God. Become wise and comfortable with God and His economy and you'll be at peace about money.

CHAPTER 5

ALL SHAKEN UP:
TURNING DOWNTURNS INTO UPTURNS

"I've heard there's going to be a recession. I've decided not to participate."
— Walt Disney

In 1928, the newly formed Walt Disney Company brought to life a whistling mouse who starred in his own feature film called *Steamboat Willie*. This precursor to the character who later would become Mickey Mouse was a smashing success and it looked like the company was poised for greatness. Less than one year later the Great Depression hit the country hard and the timing for Walt and Roy Disney's new entertainment company appeared to have been catastrophic. But as it turned out the company not only survived The Great Depression, but actually prospered. They did so for a couple of reasons.

One, they had a product no one else had. They had developed a cartoon mouse that talked and danced to music, revolutionary technology at the time. Two, their product was created for a nearly recession-proof industry. Some sectors of the entertainment business have been known to thrive during economic downturns and theirs was one of them. People were hungry—but at least during a movie they could forget about it for a couple of hours.[1]

I have experienced economic downturns and you have, too. I lived in my car and lived to tell about it. I lived through the recession of 2008 and learned to talk about it. In fact, I prospered through it. I didn't do it the way Walt Disney did, with a hand-drawn mouse or a dream for a theme park that had a train running around it.

---

1   Disney History. (n.d.). Walt Disney Archives. Retrieved from: https://d23.com/disney-history

However, both of us needed vision, and so do you.

Downturns aren't the most obvious place to find the energy for a vision. In fact, not only was I lacking a train, I barely even had a car, and the one I had doubled as my house.

During the winter of 1994 I rolled out the welcome mat and called a 1987 Nissan Sentra home. I was physically living in that car and I used to joke that it was a true motor home...it had a motor and it was my home! The motor part of my motor home didn't work so well. I would push my car, Fred Flintstones-style, to jump-start it. I would move from parking lot to parking lot and I would sleep there. I was far, far away from anything that resembled Main Street U.S.A. not to mention prosperity.

But one thing Walt and I had in common was this: I decided not to participate in the recession.

Remember that shakings are happening for you, not to you.

It was during this time that God gave me a vision of His heart. Even though He was with me, He did not want to live in my car any longer. As I began to align with God's vision to fulfill His Covenant, I came to understand God's economy and how He handles His money. I began to understand His financial system of sowing and reaping and my role in it. And I flourished.

Since that time I have come to freedom not just from the fear of economic downturns, but freedom to get really excited about them. I'm serious. Excited! God wants you to do well during these times—so you may get excited about them, too.

Shaking In Our Boots

If you've ever experienced an earthquake, tornado, or tsunami, you know they're traumatic. The shaking is loud and violent. Not all traumas are violent, though. Have you ever been living peacefully in your house, only to discover one day that termites have been stealthily using it as a buffet? Whether natural or caused by God or by us, these shaky times all have one thing in common:

They always involve money.

Recession is a natural part of the economic cycle. Sure, there are physical disasters – earthquakes, plagues, hurricanes that affect local and global economies. Most recessions, depressions, and famines are just a natural fluctuation – a financial pendulum swing. Just like in our physical bodies, when we feel pain in our economy it's because something is not right and needs to be corrected.

Though our immediate reaction in a crisis is to assume a negative outcome, we have no need to fear. These times just present us a crossroads. The term "critical care" in medicine means that a person is at a point in their illness when they're either about to die or they're about to recover. In literature, a crisis is a climactic moment that changes the direction of the story completely. The Chinese word for crisis is thought to have two pieces: one part means danger and the other means opportunity. The two parts of that one word evoke blessings ahead for those who, when things are shaken up, make the most of it.

God, too, promises shaking and blessing that are both physical and financial. God owns all wealth but it is not under His direct management.[2] Therefore, economic shake-ups are going to happen. But they do so to channel wealth back to God's vision. He gives us choice and free will, but shakings get the money back

---

2   Psalm 24:1

into the proper hands.

Remember that shakings are happening for you, not to you.

But..... The Anxiety

We've already talked about fear. Fear of talking about money, saving money, spending money, thinking about having it, thinking about not having it. You find yourself in the middle of a downturn and you wonder: what do I do about my house or my business? Should I buy? Sell? Stay still?

First, remember that money doesn't get lost it only changes hands. When income or assets decrease, they don't dissipate into thin air. That money has transferred into someone else's control.

Second, wealth is always for God's purpose. It's to fulfill His vision for mankind. God made a Covenant – a promised oath. We make covenants during recessions and downturns all the time. This all-important Abrahamic Covenant just happens to be 4000 years old and time-tested.

Third, do not fear. Anxiety is not part of the deal. Shakings are not happening to you, they're happening for you. And God's presence is the distinguishing mark in our lives. Fear not.

FAMINE: You Are More Than The News

"And you will hear wars and threats of wars, but don't panic. Yes, these things must take place, but the end won't follow immediately. Nation will go to war against nation, and kingdom against kingdom. There will be famines and earthquakes in many parts of the world." (Matthew 24:6-7, NLT)

This is from the ancient writings in the Bible, but it just as easily could have come straight from our social media news feed today. My purpose is to give you clarity and peace in this particular season. And to do that I am going to draw attention to one word from this passage:

FAMINES

I bet that's not the word you thought I'd choose in our search for clarity and peace. Famine conjures images of dust running over barren fields, children running out of Irish potatoes, and everyone running out of hope. And while all of those images can be a part of it, the actual word means something much broader.

Famine is an old English word talking about economic recession. Depression.

Why do famines occur? What are the economic shakings that rattle all industries in all nations? When famine arrives coupled with climate change (this was especially true in ancient times), the result is a depletion of our most precious commodity – water – and this sets in motion a domino effect of economic decline. In ancient times famine would have affected a region's livestock and businesses. It would have affected the transportation industry, trade, exports and imports; the entire economy. Today famine and recession affect some of these same industries.

MONEY DOESN'T GET LOST, IT ONLY CHANGES HANDS.

Discovering the truth about famine is vital to your life and wealth.

I want to remind you of God's heart for you, regardless of the economic upturns and downturns. Capturing God's heart is the key to dealing with economic uncertainty. It doesn't matter if you know the date or time or hour of an economic shift. It's more important knowing what God would have you do when shifts happen. Learn and recognize the patterns of God. What is God's intention and God's promise for you in such times?

I am not trying to predict a famine because predicting a famine isn't hard. Ancient writings, including the Bible, are full of them and they'll happen more. There's doom and gloom everywhere you go. But when you hear all of these voices, what do you do?

FAMINE IN FIVE ACTS: TWELVE WATER POTS, TWO SISTER-WIVES, SEVEN SICKLY COWS AND A FIRE

FAMINE #1: ABRAHAM

You've probably heard about Abraham. He features prominently in Jewish, Christian, and Islamic faith traditions. He had a really big family. He's one of the guys in Renaissance paintings sporting a toga and a beard. To understand how he went from living in a tent during famine to prospering during that same famine, let's introduce a little backstory.

First of all, Abraham's name was originally Abram. It would later be changed, but we will get to that in a bit. At this point in the story we'll call him Abram.

Abram and his family were living in a place called Harran, which on today's maps is considered modern-day Turkey. While Abram was living there, God told Abram and his wife, Sarai, to leave Harran and go to a land that God had promised to show him. [3] Once you get to this new land called Canaan, God said to Abram, you'll become a great nation. God promised to bless him and put his name on the map.

---

3 Acts 7:2-3 says Abram lived in Mesopotamia before Harran and that this was where he was when God appeared to him.

God told Abram that not only would He bless him and make him successful, but through his progeny Abram would also be a blessing to others. And on top of that, God promised, "I will bless those who bless you and curse those who treat you with contempt. And all the families on the earth will be blessed through you."[4]

It was quite a promise and apparently a deal Abram couldn't turn down.

Abram left Harran with his wife Sarai and his orphaned nephew, Lot, who was like the son Abram didn't yet have. Together with all of the people living with him and all of his livestock, they headed for Canaan, found an old oak tree, pitched a tent, and set up camp. It was there God appeared to him and said:

"I will give this land to your descendants." (Genesis 12:7, NLT)

Wow. Thanks for the land, God. So Abram built and dedicated an altar to God. Heading further south, they found another campground in the hills between Bethel and Ai. He built another altar and dedicated it to the Lord and worshiped there, too. This was the specific area God led him to settle in. So far, so good.

Then things got a little rough.

Famine: The F Word.

With an economic crisis gripping the nation, the large traveling caravan decided the reasonable solution was to leave Canaan and head to Egypt, the only place big enough for Abram's caravan and company to thrive.[5] Egypt was not yet affected by the recession and they would be able to participate in a larger economy there. The plan seemed fine.

Until things got a little bit weird at the border.

---
4 Genesis 12:1-3
5 Genesis 12:10

"We should pretend you're my sister," he said to his wife.

Your sister?

"Here's the thing, Sarai. You are really pretty. And these guys do not look stupid. I'm afraid that they are going to take one look at you and want you for themselves. Which means I'm going to be taken out into some dark Egyptian alley and never be seen or heard from again and then they will have you for their own. So here's my plan: we'll just tell them that you're my sister. That's right. That sounds good. And then because they are so taken with you, they'll not only let me live but they'll treat me well, too."[6]

Smooth talker.

Why in the world would he go to such an extreme? Abram had already received a vision from God. He knew that through him all nations of the earth would be blessed. He was already wealthy with servants and employees and vehicles of donkeys and cattle. He had faith in this future vision that would reach all nations, so he should have felt pretty confident. He had a big God, a bunch of possessions, and a big traveling party. God has just appeared to him and showed him the land that was his to flourish in. But instead he took off running from the news of famine and lied to the King, hoping that Egypt would be the solution.

Basically, he panicked.

We all have a tendency to panic. Still, for a while Abram's plan worked as he had hoped. Sarai was taken to Pharaoh with her husband-brother scurrying giddily in tow. And they were both given many gifts – sheep, goats, cattle, donkeys, servants, and camels. The works.

But the truth would eventually come out.

When Pharaoh found out about Abram and Sarai, he kicked

---

6 Genesis 12:11-13

them out. And because Pharaoh was nervous about the curse Abram and Sarai had apparently brought with them, they got to go free. Plus, they got to take all their stuff with them. And in case we had lost track of the money situation, they were already rich in livestock, silver, and gold when they arrived in Egypt. But they left Egypt with even more silver, gold, and livestock and became very rich.[7]

Realignment: Time To Go Back To Bethel

Things eventually worked out really well for Abram, but the resolution to this part of the story may seem strange to you.

Abram goes to Egypt, which is not where he was supposed to go in the first place, and then worsens things by lying about his sister-wife. But even in the face of famine, uncertainty, and dishonesty, God still blesses him. That's shocking to religious people because it's not legalistic, as some would have liked it to be.

But Abram hadn't yet heard about the Law of Moses, about all of the rules that would come around 400 years later. He only knew about a loving God who had a vision and Abram was making room for God's vision in his life. In this case famine was just a cycle in the economy; there isn't an indication that it was brought about by God.

The reason God took care of Abram in Egypt was because Abram was in Covenant with God. The blessing was working in his life from the day he first heard the gospel—God's vision for future generations to come. The ideal environment for the blessing to thrive is one of grace. In the midst of uncertainty and in the midst of his own developing faith, God graciously blessed him financially.

---

7   Genesis 13:1-2

So Abram and his giant tribe of people and storehouses of wealth packed up and left Egypt and went right back to Bethel, to the same place God showed him, where he built the altar. Despite the famine, this time around their possessions, business, and livestock grew and were so great that they couldn't all occupy the land together. There was too much stuff, too much prosperity, too much of everything. And because of the lack of adequate space, Abram's and Lot's employees started fighting.

Shakings Always Precede Divine Alignment

Abram came up with a solution. He told his nephew, Lot, to look around and pick a spot in Canaan for him and his family to live. Abram would take the rest. Lot chose Sodom which—despite what we know and think of now as the Sodom of up-in-smoke Sodom and Gomorrah fame—was a lush green area. It was the most fertile land there was.

> **THE IDEAL ENVIRONMENT FOR THE BLESSING TO THRIVE IS ONE OF GRACE.**

Then a funny thing happened. Once Lot headed out for Sodom, Abram could hear and see God more clearly. Lot's name means veil, and now the veil was gone. Lot wasn't supposed to be there in the first place and his presence diminished Abram's ability to hear God distinctly, or to see the next steps in the big picture. God was speaking, it's just that Abram couldn't see or hear him well, while Lot was there.

Now that Abram was in line with the vision that God had for him, it was time for a name change. Sarai was going to get a new name, too.

God didn't want him to be Abram—whose name means "exalted

father"—any longer. He wanted him to be Abraham—"father of many nations," and Sarai would become Sarah—"mother of many nations."[8] Abram had tried to take on his fatherhood role in the form of Lot's family but that locked things up a bit. God's plan was WAY bigger. He wanted Abraham to be the father of many nations. God's plan for Abraham's personal life was much larger than what could be imagined and it's also part of God's plan for all of us.

In times of uncertainty and famine, there is only one goal that God has – to get you in line with His corporate plan and His vision. And you aren't to be afraid of famine if you are walking with God because He is getting ready to flourish you in the time of famine. It is an opportunity to a turn a downturn into an upturn. Remember: shakings are happening for you, not to you.

Wrong Relationships Need To Be Re-Aligned In Times Of Uncertainty

Sometimes God's plan includes a shaking of relationships.

It's in times of uncertainty that we realize who should and shouldn't be in our lives. Abram's intentions with Lot were out of love – he wanted to replace Lot's dead father and Abram didn't have any children. It seemed like a good solution. He just didn't know God had a bigger plan.

Three things happened here—things that always happen in times of economic uncertainty. First, God revived and renewed His vision. Second, He moved wealth into its proper place and His people prospered. God wants us to financially multiply during times of uncertainty by purposely participating and establishing His vision. Money is never lost, it just changes hands. Third, God aligns our relationships through the process. This certainly happened to Abraham. God revived and renewed His vision for Abraham's life, and the famine shifted into an upturn in wealth, relationships, and vision for God's purpose.

---

8 Genesis 17:15

Abraham would have liked Walt Disney because, like him, Abraham didn't participate in the recession, either. He actually prospered!

The famine of Abraham's day was behind them, but little did the family know that another one was on the way. Abraham's son, Isaac, was about to learn that as much as famine affects the sons of their fathers, wealth would be for the next generation, too.

FAMINE #2: ISAAC

Isaac is remembered for a couple of things besides being the miracle son of elderly parents. For one, he was offered as a sacrifice to God. Literally. When Isaac was a boy, Abraham was asked by God to offer his own son as a light-a-fire-atop-a-pile-of-wood sacrifice. Trusting God, Abraham packed up his boy, strapped some wood to his back, and carried a torch and a knife and they headed up the mountain together.

Somewhere along the journey Isaac looked around, suspicious that they were missing the most important element of the sacrifice – the animal.

"So, uh, Dad, uh, where's the lamb we are going to sacrifice?"

Abraham said, "God is going to provide it." And then he built an altar. And Abraham laid Isaac on top of the altar.

As he pulled his knife back to slay his son, something stopped him.

And then—

At that moment the angel of the Lord called to him from heaven, "Abraham! Abraham!" "Yes," Abraham replied. "Here I am! Don't lay a hand on the boy!" The angel said. "Do not hurt him in any way, for now I know that you truly fear

God. You have not withheld from me even your son, your only son." (Gen 22:11-12, NLT)

God provided a ram as a sacrifice and Abraham offered it to God in place of his son. He named the place "the Lord Will Provide."[9] God confirmed the Covenant by an oath to Abraham, reiterating that because of his faith he would be blessed and that his many descendants would also be blessed.

Now on to the descendants.

Abraham died at age 175 and God blessed Isaac.[10] Abraham had left the family in good shape but now, despite the inherited wealth of his father, Isaac was faced with a famine of his own. In an effort to problem-solve like his dad, Isaac started walking toward Egypt: Land of Opportunity. God stepped in, though, and reminded him no:

"Live here as a foreigner in this land, and I will be with you and bless you. I hereby confirm that I will give all these lands to you and your descendants, just as I solemnly promised to Abraham, your father. I will cause your descendants to become as numerous as the stars of the sky, and I will give them all these lands. And through your descendants all of the earth will be blessed." (Genesis 26: 2-4, NLT)

Why is God intervening? Because of the vision He shared with Abraham and the oath He made to continue that vision through Isaac and his progeny. He is now continuing that vision. Isaac is getting and following instruction from the Holy Spirit. So he listens and he stays in Gerar. God gives us, too, specific instruction on how to participate in His vision because we are continuing in that living relationship with Him.

---

9 Genesis 22:14
10 Genesis 25:11

Sow Seed In The Ground

Isaac followed God's direction and with time now on his hands in Canaan, he started sowing seeds into the completely dry ground.

Sowing seed in dry ground may seem like no big deal, but in truth Isaac was doing something completely crazy here. He took seed and sowed it into ground where naturally there would be no hope of a harvest.

Isaac worked against the recession mentality. You know the one. We want to save our seed instead of sowing the seed we've been given to sow. Remember; never sow your bread and never eat your seed. Isaac sowed and God blessed him 100-fold (10,000%).[11] That is supernatural. Remember that the blessing that had been working in Abraham's life and in Isaac's life is also working in your life.

Economic shifts don't determine what happens to you. For instance, when people are afraid they tend to back away from things. But that's where we can buy and invest. Every time people have "lost" money, someone is making money. The media is teaching you fear, and the worldly economy hopes you will buy it, because fear paralyzes. But love mobilizes. God wants you to act according to His Spirit.

Isaac continued prospering until he became VERY wealthy.[12] He was so prosperous that he incited fear and jealousy among the Philistines and his other neighbors. The Philistines filled the Israelites' wells with earth, hoping they would leave. Even King Abimelech wanted them to leave because he was jealous.

Isaac returned again to dig the ancient wells that Abraham built and that the Philistines had filled, and every time he dug a well he found running water. He kept digging. Not only was he prospering on his own, but he was also claiming the generational wealth of his father.

---

11 Genesis 26:6-12
12 Genesis 26:6-14

Generational Inheritance and Personal Wealth

Why was Isaac continuing to prosper? Because God absolutely intends for us to thrive in times of economic shakings so we can establish His Covenant and get the gospel out. When you hear doom and gloom it's time to get excited!

Later King Abimelech would come back and acknowledge that Isaac served the one true God. He didn't want to mess with Isaac's God. When you prosper, people will get in your way but keep going.... because God is at work. Eventually, even enemies will align. This treaty of peace between Isaac and his enemies was a powerful blessing.

Isaac kept on planting despite King Abimelech's opposition to Isaac's family. God's plan was for His Covenant with Abraham to be fulfilled. An imperfect follower, an unhappy king, and a big old recession were not going to stand in the way of that.

Isaac listened to the Spirit. He sowed his seed in fallow ground and God prospered him. Isaac multiplied his revenue streams and received his father's inheritance...all during a famine. This wealth was preserved for Abraham, Isaac, and even Jacob, as you will see later. Not only did God prosper him, but He promised wealth to future generations.

There were going to be a lot of future generations, too. Isaac's son, Jacob, had twelve sons and one of them, a dreamer named Joseph, was set to bring their family out of another, even greater, famine into Egypt.

FAMINE #3: JOSEPH

The famines in the time of Abraham and Isaac were somewhat regional, but by the time Joseph makes it onto the scene there was another recession and it was big. This was a global famine, and God was setting the stage for a global alignment.

You'll remember that Joseph was the kid with the colorful coat. He gets thrown down a well and sold into slavery by his jealous brothers before they returned home to tell their father, Jacob, "sorry, dad, your favorite kid seems to have been eaten by lions."[13] After some time in the well, Joseph was picked up by Ishmaelite travelers who sold him as a slave to Potiphar, Pharaoh's right-hand man.

Despite some early setbacks, Joseph did well working for Potiphar and the Pharaoh. They realized that God was with Joseph and they gave him charge over a lot of important things.

Later Potiphar's wife tried to seduce this now-older and attractive Joseph. Things ended badly and Joseph found himself in prison. God had a plan, though. Joseph could interpret dreams and, as God would have it, the Pharaoh was having some big ones.

God Speaks to Authorities First

One night, Pharaoh dreamt that there were seven fat cows and seven skinny cows all standing in a field together. The skinny cows turned around and ate all of the fat cows. Startled, Pharaoh woke up. When he returned back to sleep, he again dreamt, this time that there were seven tall, healthy stalks of grain growing in a field next to seven withering ones and, similar to the cows, the sickly stalks of grain ate the big ones. What was he to make of this?

Joseph was summoned out of prison to interpret Pharaoh's dreams. Both dreams have the same interpretation, Joseph said: seven years of prosperity will be followed by years of famine. You'll need to start storing provisions away, he said.

---

13 Genesis 37

Because of Joseph's consistently sound advice, he was made second in charge of everything Pharaoh owned. This was not a bad gig for a guy who just got out of prison.

As the years of plenty came to an end and the years of famine began, everyone in Egypt panicked. They didn't know how they were going to eat. The only option was to sell their land to Pharaoh. And when they sold their land Joseph made them a deal. He gave them seed to grow on their now-rented land. In return, he told them, Pharaoh would receive 20% of all the crops grown on the land and they could keep the remaining 80% to use as both food for themselves and seed for their crops. They were thrilled. This saved their lives. So, they replanted the seed for future crops and had bread for their families to eat.[14]

Meanwhile, Pharaoh prospered because Joseph, a man chosen four generations earlier as the seed promised to Abraham, was aligning with God's plan. God made Egypt an economic superpower and He did that so that one day a pharaoh would rise up and God would be able to show Himself as mightier than the greatest leader of the most powerful nation on earth.

God always intended for Joseph to go into Egypt because He had a global plan in place to get the vision into all the corners of the earth. And for that Covenant to be established He was about to financially bless Joseph in the midst of considerable economic uncertainty.

God Preserves Generational Wealth

Now back to the story...

Joseph sent his brothers and his father, Jacob, to dwell in Goshen, the best land in the whole world. Joseph explained God's plan to his brothers:

---

14 Genesis: Chapters 39-41

"But now, do not therefore be grieved or angry with yourselves because you sold me here; for God sent me before you to preserve life. For these two years the famine has been in the land, and there are still five years in which there will be neither plowing nor harvesting. And God sent me before you to preserve a posterity for you in the earth, and to save your lives by a great deliverance." (Genesis 45:5-7, NKJV)

There was personal wealth for Joseph, and there was wealth for big old Pharaoh. But there was also generational wealth. Joseph's father, Jacob, also prospered in the famine. The newly-minted people of Israel prospered, too. All of Jacob's cattle that had been preserved was taken into Egypt and multiplied over time. They would have all the Egyptians' cattle, too. They sowed their seed and acquired property. They were fruitful and their population grew rapidly.

When There's Famine In The World...MULTIPLY!

The nation of Israel dwelt in Goshen. They grew and multiplied exceedingly. Part of the blessing of God was the multiplication. God wants you to sow and multiply, too.

God used Pharaoh. He is a respector of authority and because of Joseph's alignment with God's vision during a time of famine, God used Pharaoh and the wealth in the entire region multiplied.

But not everyone saw this as a good thing.

FAMINE #4 MOSES

The Hebrew people were once again looking at a downturn. They had now grown powerful and had so multiplied in number that the new Pharaoh was threatened. The new Pharaoh didn't remember Joseph and how the Israelites' God had saved the day for Egypt. Instead he was paranoid and hostile.

As their numbers grew, Pharaoh began a systematic enslavement of the Israelite people. God prospered them anyway and this made Pharaoh even more angry. The only way to take them down, he decided, was to start killing babies. He killed the firstborn male in every Hebrew household. He was nuts.

"And God heard their groaning, and he remembered his covenant promise to Abraham, Isaac, and Jacob. He looked down on the people of Israel and knew it was time to act." (Exodus 2:24-25, NLT)

Moses started life floating in a basket, grew up in Pharaoh's house, killed an Egyptian guard, and one day found himself in front of a burning bush that talked. It was there in front of the burning bush that God gave him a big job to do. God told Moses:

"I have certainly seen the oppression of my people in Egypt. I have heard their cries of distress because of their harsh slave drivers. Yes, I am aware of their suffering. So I have come down to rescue them from the power of the Egyptians and lead them out of Egypt into their own fertile and spacious land. It is a land flowing with milk and honey.... Now go, for I am sending you to Pharaoh. You must lead my people Israel out of Egypt." (Exodus 3:7-10, NLT)

God had a plan and he wanted to use Moses. "I will stretch out my hand and strike Egypt with all my wonders. I will give these people favors and you will not go empty handed."[15] God used miracles and wonders and, when those didn't work, plagues.

Why did God care if they were empty-handed or not? It was because God had a plan.

What was God's plan? God was going to move money and then move people. God had been working on this for 400+ years. Moses showed up as part of the plan to transfer wealth by getting all the cattle and livestock plus all the gold and silver in Egypt.

---

15 Exodus 3:20-21

How did they get it? They followed God's instruction and just asked.

Moses and the Israelites prospered in Egypt. Now that the plagues were over, Pharaoh asked them to please go and take all their belongings with them. They gathered all their stuff and on the way out they asked the Egyptians for their clothing and articles of silver and gold. In fact, the Egyptians gave the Israelites everything they asked for. The Israelites stripped the Egyptians of their wealth.

God's people experienced a tremendous upturn here. It was just as God had promised four generations earlier.[16] In fact, they left Egypt with an entire national economy. Experts say that the sum of this wealth is nearly immeasurable, that there aren't enough zeros on a page. And if you think this was the stuff of biblical urban legend, both the Jews and the Egyptians are still very much talking about it in the 21st Century.[17]

Remember, in a time of recession: The greater the downturn, the greater the other side of the equation for God's people to prosper. There is a boom for God's people on the other side of the doom and gloom.

FAMINE #5: ELIJAH

Abraham, Isaac, Jacob, and Joseph survived and prospered during what were largely natural economic downturns. Moses survived mass genocide and went on not only to free people from slavery but to prosper them. God used economic instability to move the wealth back into alignment with His vision and with His purpose. He even used unbelievers like Pharaoh to make it happen.

---

16 Genesis 15:14
17 Ghitis, F. (2003). Dragging Moses into a lawsuit. Chicago Tribune. Retrieved from: http://articles.chicagotribune.com/2003-08-31/news/0308310131_1_egyptian-jews-moses

Sometimes, though, the realignment happens in a full-on battle between the economic powers. Enter King Ahab and his evil sidekick, Queen Jezebel.

This famine was because of idolatry and poor leadership. King Ahab was the worst king to ever live and he was married to Jezebel who was the worst queen to ever live. Through the worship of Baal/Satan, she made her wealth. She trusted in Baal as the god of economy. As a result, God brought about a drought and, because water was the chief commodity, it dried up the land and then the entire economy. This was the great "God vs. Mammon" showdown!

There is a boom for God's people on the other side of the doom and gloom.

You can make your wealth worshiping Satan or worshiping God. You must make your choice. Baal was the god of the weather and economy, and because the people, most notably their leaders, were so taken with him, there was a severe drought in the land.

God's prophets in the Old Testament would carry the mantle of economy, too. Why was the rain important? It controlled the economy. Jezebel thought the economy was controlled by her idols. God was going to shake up Baal and the spirit of Mammon and He would give the people an option to make a choice.

And He was going to use the prophet Elijah to get it done.

Widows Waiting for Rain

God spoke to Elijah and said,

> *"Go and live in the village of Zarephath, near the city of Sidon. I have instructed a widow there to feed you." (1Kings 17:9, NLT)*

Elijah found the widow and asked her to give him a piece of bread and something to drink.

As is usually the case when we are down to our last of anything, the widow was reluctant to feed Elijah. "I'm down to my very last bit of flour and oil," she said. "I don't know how I am going to feed my son after today." Elijah promised her, though, that there would be oil and flour in her house and that her containers would never be empty. In fact, they ate for three years and never ran out.[18]

When sometime later the boy died of disease, Elijah laid himself over the child's body and the child returned to life.

> *"Then the woman told Elijah, 'Now I know for sure that you are a man of God, and that the LORD truly speaks through you.'" (1 Kings 17:24, NLT)*

By feeding Elijah first a portion of her only cake, the widow was blessed for herself, her son, and all her servants for three years. What she thought was bread to eat was also seed to sow. In other words, by giving him literal bread she was sowing seed for her future. God multiplied her bread. She was a Gentile – not even in Covenant with God – but because she aligned with God's vision, the widow prospered in famine. She invested in God's plan. She made room for God's vision and God made room for her in His vision.

CHARIOTS AND FIRE

At this time, many of the Lord's prophets were imprisoned or dead and Elijah's name and his God's greatness had been spreading throughout the region. And the king and queen were not happy about it.

---

18 1 Kings 15-17

It was time for a showdown.

Elijah and King Ahab agreed to meet at Mount Carmel. With them, Ahab and Jezebel summon the 450 prophets of Baal and the 400 prophets of Asherah, as well as the entire nation of Israel for a showdown over the economy.

The gauntlet was laid: Each side would build an altar and slaughter a bull for a sacrifice. Whichever side's God was the first to show up by fire would be considered the one true God.

The prophets of Baal did all kinds of crazy things to get that fire going – cutting, prophesying, dancing, flag waving – but nothing. No one paid attention. Even today people are walking around with Baal prophecy. This kind of prophecy seduces the soul into idolatry rather than serving God.

Elijah took twelve water pots (incidentally, twelve is the number of Jacob's sons) and filled them with water. He took the most precious commodity there was – water – and made an offering to the Lord. He dumped twelve pots all over the wood and then summoned God to light it anyway. God lit a fire so hot that not only did it burn the wood and the bull, but it instantly licked up all the water poured out from the pots.

By sowing a seed of water, the most valuable commodity, Elijah shifted the economy.

"Seize the prophets of Baal," Elijah said. And then he killed them all.

Turning back to King Ahab he said, "Your prophets are dead and there's rain coming. You'd better head home." As they headed home, a cloud came up out of the sea and the heavens opened with a rain so heavy that even the chariots couldn't outrun it.

Elijah had come with the mantle of God's economy and defeated the prophets of Baal and Satan's economy. Elijah had prophesied for the rain to come, so when it was his turn to light the fire he did so by first dumping water on the wood. God lit the fire anyway. Sowing the seed of water as an offering onto the water-soaked, hard-to-light pile of wood unlocked the economy and released the rain. God again multiplied seed into its own likeness. Water into water. The widow's bread into food. The famine was over.

Wealth Comes Before Glory: Whom Will You Serve?

I believe God is judging the world's system, just as in the days of Elijah. Many of you who are following God thrived during the last recession. My wife and I did. We sold our house two weeks before the crash and bought another two weeks after. I want you to prosper, too. Look at God's heart in this process; it will eliminate all fear.

In the years since, God has been asking people to make a choice about whom they will serve. This means that if you've been participating with God you're in for a major, major harvest, especially in times of famine.

Will every Christian automatically prosper? Absolutely not, but when you do, you can be a conduit for others to prosper. We can help our family. God's purpose is always for you to fulfill your assignment, which is connected to His vision. Don't underestimate yourself! God has a sovereign purpose concerning you.

He might physically move you or ask you to sell things or buy things, but you'll never be afraid. He will set your mind free from the demonic doctrine of a monastic tradition that says God wants you poor. He doesn't want you to have money just to keep it and do whatever you want with it, but he does want you to use it to establish the Abrahamic Covenant and His vision for all mankind.

There's going to be an incredible release of wealth in these days ahead and God says we are to steward it so we can steward souls and all heavenly riches, including the glory. He releases His wealth before He releases His glory, so if you can steward His wealth (which is something you see that is natural) then you can steward the glory of God.[19]

This is the pattern of God – in the worst of times God will make it the best of times for you. Shakings precede the best of times.

REVISITING THE COVENANT

Today, it's a brand new season altogether. It's more important to do what God is saying than trying to predict what is going to happen. Are you going to be positioned to apply what God is doing? If so, you're going to see the greatest harvest on the planet since the cross. And this harvest is the good news to all mankind.

In Hebrews 6:13-20 God made a promise and an oath.

"For when God made a promise to Abraham, because He could swear by no one greater, He swore by Himself, saying, 'Surely blessing I will bless you, and multiplying I will multiply you.' And so, after he had patiently endured, he obtained the promise. For men indeed swear by the greater, and an oath for confirmation is for them an end of all dispute. Thus God, determining to show more abundantly to the heirs of promise the immutability of His counsel, confirmed it by an oath, that by two immutable things, in which it is impossible for God to lie, we might[b] have strong consolation, who have fled for refuge to lay hold of the hope set before us.

---

19 Luke 16:11

This hope we have as an anchor of the soul, both sure and steadfast, and which enters the Presence behind the veil, where the forerunner has entered for us, even Jesus, having become High Priest forever according to the order of Melchizedek." (Hebrews 6:13-20, NKJV)

The promise was to bless and multiply your descendants beyond number. God cannot lie so He bound himself to the Covenant. And Abraham waited patiently. God's oath binds Himself to His promise to Abraham. Abraham and his descendants (that's us, too) can be assured that God will never change his mind.

The result of this is HOPE. Hope is strong. The book of Hebrews says that even when there is no reason for hope, it is a trustworthy anchor for our souls. Hope leads us through the curtain into God's inner sanctuary. Jesus, our high priest, has already led the way there.[20]

Walt Disney had a recession-proof mouse that brought people from depression to a happy place where there were no downturns or famines or litter or insects or ice cream that melts. But while the vision is good, the train goes in circles.

God's vision is perfect and it always moves us forward. Shakings are just part of the momentum.

Shakings realign money and relationships. They precede wealth transfers for those who participate in God's vision and a release of God's glory for those who have learned to steward wealth. It involves planting seeds, digging wells, and starting fires with twelve buckets of water. And sometimes it involves a pharaoh or two.

And if you must turn on the news remember that you are more than what they're telling you. Fear paralyzes, but love mobilizes. Go forth and multiply!

---

20 Hebrews 6:198

CHAPTER 6

TAKING IT TO THE BANK:
WISE INVESTING

*"Rule Number One: Never lose money.
Rule Number 2: Never forget Rule Number One."*

Warren Buffett

Warren Buffett once said that someone's sitting in the shade today because someone else planted a tree a long time ago. In his case, the shade tree he was sitting under was likely to have had gum stuck to it.

In 1936, chewing gum was a big black market industry for six-year-olds. And the kids couldn't have been happier about it. Especially one kid.

At six years old, Warren Buffett sold packages of Juicy Fruit gum for profit on the playground. And when the weather warmed up, he switched gears and sold bottles of discounted Coca-Cola that he had purchased at his grandfather's store. With a going rate of five cents apiece, this boy still missing his two front teeth was shrewd enough to pocket two cents for every sale. He bought low and sold high. He made a seed investment to reap a generous return.

By the time Buffett was 11, he made his first stock market investment- three shares of stock for $27 each.

Time didn't slow him down, either. When Warren Buffett was 50 years old he had $1/100^{th}$ of the amount of money he has now. He knew what he was doing and he didn't waste any time. He increased his wealth one hundred-fold during the autumn of his life – a time when many people are beginning to financially coast.[1]

Needless to say, people hang onto his every word. And when looking for financial advice, everyone always seems to have the same question for him:

What makes a good investor?

Preaching a gospel of value-based investing, Warren Buffett became one of the greatest investors of all time. He started at age 11 with $100 and turned it into more than $76 billion dollars and growing.[2] So, what makes a good investor? Among the many principles he set forth for investing, some of the biggest ones are these.[3]

- Buy Within a Margin of Safety

- Invest with Favorable Long-term Prospects

- Evaluate Management by Reputation

- Invest Within Your Circle of Confidence

Let's explore these for a minute.

Buy Within a Margin of Safety

When stock, real estate, or your cold medicine is discounted, buy it. Purchase an item worth ten dollars for five dollars, and then invest the savings. It's not just buy low and sell high. "Price is

---

[1] 1936-2013. (2013). The Evolution of Warren Buffett's Career. Old School Value. Retrieved from: https://www.oldschoolvalue.com/blog/investing-perspective/warren-buffett-career-timeline-investments
[2] Profile (2017). Profile/Warren Buffett. Forbes Media LLC. Retrieved from https://www.forbes.com/profile/warren-buffett/
[3] John. (2016). The 4 Warren Buffett Stock Investing Principles. Vintage Value Investing. Retrieved from: http://vintagevalueinvesting.com/the-4-warren-buffett-stock-investing-principles/

what you pay; value is what you get," Buffet reminds us. It's also about the value of what you do with the money you save from the original purchase. When you buy at a discount invest the savings and you will build value on both the purchase and on the savings!

INVEST WITH FAVORABLE LONGTERM PROSPECTS.

Warren Buffett reminds us that "time is the friend of the wonderful company, the enemy of the mediocre." Why do we need time? Because money naturally fluctuates and changes hands, and there is a patience associated with the type of investing that will return the most value.

EXPECT VOLATILITY

Not only that, but profit from it. Use downturns in the market as an opportunity to find well-priced investments. And then when it gets overvalued, sell it! Instead of following what someone else – the media, the demon on your shoulder, or the father-in-law in your living room – tells you to do when the market gets stressful, make the most of volatility. Volatility is your friend. The key is always to look long-term. By long-term I mean whatever length of time it takes for your seed to produce fruit. That may be two days or ten years. But if you wouldn't want to still own it in ten years to see the fruit, don't buy it today. Be patient.

EVALUATE MANAGEMENT BY REPUTATION

This is pretty straightforward. Do you trust your investment will be in good hands and good is going to come from it? Does the company have a history of fraud or shady dealings? Would you trust your future and your family's future to the way its run?

INVEST WITHIN YOUR CIRCLE OF COMPETENCE.

In other words, know what kind of investor you are. And then invest in a business you understand. "You don't have to be an expert on every company, or even many," Buffet says. But you do need to know about who and what you are investing in. And you need to know yourself, too.

How much time do you really want to invest in managing your money? Do you love to watch your investments? Do you like to pay someone else to watch them? Be wise, in other words. Know your limits and know what your level of competence and your personality will allow you to do.

We are talking about real money and how to spend it. We know what Warren Buffett says. You likely also know what your father-in-law and the guy making a big commission at your friend's brokerage all say.

We also know that the purpose of wealth is to align with God's vision and fulfill His Covenant, and that money is as spiritual as it is physical. We also know that God's economy works within the regular economy.

So, does traditional investment wisdom work in God's banking system?

KNOW YOUR ECONOMIC GODS

First, let's define a few things.

What is meant by the term *"banking system"*?

A banking system is a network that provides financial services for us. It processes deposits and withdrawals, helps with investing, and issues loans to consumers. Both businesses and individuals operate within a banking system, and the place to operate locally within the global banking system is at a branch.

If you're going to make an investment through a physical bank, you have some options: big, small, local, overseas, one that gives great advice, or one that hands out free toasters. There are literally thousands of choices.

Money is as much spiritual as it is physical, and as important as it is to take our money out from under our mattress and deposit it in a bank down the street, we also need to figure out how we are investing real money into a larger economic system. And when it comes to investing money in an economic system, we only have two choices:

We can choose God's Banking System or Mammon's Banking System.

"...choose today whom you will serve." (Joshua 24:15, NLT)

Money is as much spiritual as it is physical.

The Bank of Mammon

Mammon is the love of the money itself and is built on the belief that money supplies and satisfies your needs. Mammon's bank is based on a "buy-sell" economy. It's self-serving. The person who gains is always you.

Money in Mammon's bank is subject to theft, fire, and inflation.[4]

The Bank of God

In God's banking system, the money you have (make, give, and invest) is for His purpose. The money is all His. And the movement of money is an opportunity to return God's money back into His economy. God's banking process is based on

---

4 Matthew 6:19

"sowing and reaping." God gives you "seed" for investing in His economy, and He provides "bread" to satisfy your needs.

The Apostle Paul explains the seed sowing system this way:

"Now he who supplies seed to the sower and bread for food will also supply and increase your store of seed and will enlarge the harvest of your righteousness." (2 Corinthians 9:10, NIV)

What's the difference?

The difference begins with God's economy working inside of the world's economy.

In aerodynamics, the law of lift allows for the force of motion to keep a very heavy airplane in the air. In doing so, lift is able to supersede the law of gravity. Gravity still exists, but something with greater power allows a 500-passenger 747 to get away from it.

Similarly, God's economy supersedes the world's economy. God uses real money in the real world but it operates a bigger cause within it. God's economy functions in this world but is not of it. And because it is not bound by the world's standards, it is inflation-proof, theft-proof and fireproof.

God's system works within the worldly system. It isn't completely separate. Your choice between the two is very important because whichever system you participate in will become your master. If you serve God, money will serve you. If you exclusively participate in the worldly economy – if you serve mammon – then money will rule over you.

"No one can serve two masters. Either you will hate the one and love the other, or you will be devoted to the one and despise the other. You cannot serve both God and money." (Luke 16:13, NIV)

What this comes down to is a heavenly banking system vs. a worldly banking system. In Mammon's economy, you put your treasure in the worldly system. You build wealth exclusively based on debit/credit and buy/sell. This means you desire and trust money, and you pursue it for your own personal gain.

God's banking system is part of a heavenly economy. It has a guaranteed return on investment. All the money in your hand is for you to steward and to make choices with. Your stewardship – how you take care of what's been entrusted to you—fits into three categories: Tithe, Seed and Bread.

INVESTING, FARMING AND WHY YOU DON'T PLANT BREAD IN THE SPRING

So we are choosing a banking system. Most of us understand how buying and selling and debit and credit work. But God's system is different. Let's define these terms.

THE TITHE

The tithe is one-tenth, the first tenth, of income that is returned to God.

Tithing is a token of honor of your Covenant with God. It is like the "wedding ring" of your Covenant and just like a wedding ring is the symbol of a marriage, tithing is an earthly representation of a heavenly concept. Tithing is not something we give to God; It is something we return to Him because money is all His.

Tithing is important because it keeps us connected. This is the channel to the flow of resources, wealth, and supply going into the House of God and then into the local church. For example, Wells Fargo is a bank, a part of a banking system. And just as when a banking contract is exercised, this is where money changes hands. We mentioned earlier that to participate in that banking system you use a branch. The church is the central hub and branch of the heavenly banking system.

THE SEED

After the tithe, what remains is seed and bread. Giving (sowing seed) begins after returning the tithe and is over and above the tithe. The seed is supplied by God and sown by you. What is the impact of the seed? It's an investment. It's capital for your future. Wherever it is sown it is multiplied in impact and return. In a letter to the church at Corinth, the apostle Paul explained the seed further this way:

"For God is the one who provides seed for the farmer and then bread to eat. In the same way, he will provide and increase your resources and then produce a great harvest of generosity in you. Yes, you will be enriched in every way so that you can always be generous. And when we take your gifts to those who need them, they will thank God." (II Corinthians 9:10-11, NLT)

Notice the seed precedes the bread.

THE BREAD

The bread is everything you need in your life on earth from houses to cars to the best education for your kids. Bread is also for your investments, business, and livelihood. Not everyone starts with the same amount of bread. God supplies it just like He supplies the seed. And He says don't worry about it.

God provides the seed. It's the seed that is the investment strategy of God's economic system. In the same way that you never sow your bread, you never eat your seed.

HOW DOES THE SYSTEM WORK?

To illustrate how the system works, we'll use an example. For ease, let's say we made $100.

First, Return Tithe

From this income we first return the tithe, which is 10% and goes into the house of God. This tells God, "We know this came from you. In doing this we are confirming Jesus as the High priestly fulfillment of the Abrahamic Covenant."[5]

So, the first thing we do with our $100 is return $10 in tithe.

Tithing is returning back to God out of honor. When you begin to honor God by tithing, you begin to redeem money from the spirit of Mammon attached to it. God opens doors for you that no one can shut.

The tithe is not the seed and the seed is not the tithe. The tithe doesn't multiply, but instead unlocks every promise of God. While tithe brings the Covenant, it is the seed that unlocks multiplication.

Enter the seed and the bread.

Second, Decide what is seed and what is bread

We have $90 left. Some of this is bread, the stuff we need, and some of it is seed, the part we invest, or sow. How do we know what is seed and what is bread? Through both practice and spiritual discernment. By practicing sowing seed and asking the Spirit to lead you, you will begin to get a sense of how much of what is provided to you is seed and how much is bread. Then sow the seed and live on the bread. Don't be afraid to make a mistake. God will honor your journey. My suggestion is to start sowing in

---

5 Hebrews 4:14

increments of 10% over and above your tithe. So out of the $90 sow $10, $20 or $30. Over time you will be able to increase the measure of what you can sow in God's economy as it multiplies in impact and return.

Third, Sow Seed

There are several principals to seed multiplication.

First, remember that seed multiplies and produces its own kind. Apple seeds grow apple trees and these trees produce more fruit and more seeds. People produce more people, who are both the fruit of two people, but also a fruit with their own seed. And money reaps more money. Investing money does not produce a dog. It multiplies back in the form of money that has changed hands from somewhere else, but now belongs to you.

Second, seed always reaps more than we sow. An apple seed doesn't produce one new apple with one seed. It produces hundreds, even thousands that can either be eaten or re-sown. Populations continue to increase because people are created with the ability to reproduce many-fold. As a human race, we aren't just reproducing ourselves. We are multiplying.

Third, God provides the seed and only multiplies the seed that is sown. It is the seed that, when sown, produces wealth in the form of capital, descendants or apples. It's not a gambling system; it's a heart system. Sowing and reaping is so powerful that it extends beyond money!

Fourth, Consistent Practice

This lifestyle is a process and when you practice it consistently you'll find that your tithe will increase, your seed will increase, and your bread will increase over time.

Its important to note the multiplication process is supernatural because of the blessing upon your seed. This blessing will continue to harvest results in the real world, in your family and business and life in general.

Finally, it is for everyone.

A quick look at how farming, human reproduction, and investing work, and we know that the sowing and reaping economy works for all of us.

KIDS, REAL ESTATE, AND HOW NOT TO GO HUNGRY

For examples of how this works, we are going to look at several people with very different amounts and types of seed to sow. All were multiplied in nearly immeasurable ways.

Once Upon A Time there was a boy with some lunch

Picture yourself at a mega-conference, except that instead of gathering in the conference room at the Marriott you're sitting on a hillside listening to Jesus.

There is a large crowd gathered around as Jesus delivers His keynote address, and by midday the people are getting hungry. So the disciples, big event planners that they were, started coming up with a plan.

"Maybe we should break for dinner. Everyone can head into the city – we've made some deals with a few local restaurants and the owners are expecting you. For those of you wishing to do fast food, that works, too. Enjoy your nice sit-down lunches or grab your extra value meals, but either way session two begins promptly at seven, so make sure you're back in time."

But Jesus had another plan.

"You guys feed them," He said.[6]

"Come on, Jesus, we've worked out a plan. We even organized it. And most importantly, we don't have any food and to go buy food for several thousand people, especially at the last minute, is REALLY expensive. You don't want us wasting money, do you?"

The disciples were worried about money. But when Jesus said, "feed them," He meant in His economy.

Jesus also tested Philip, one of the disciples, to see where his head was at:

"Then Jesus lifted up His eyes, and seeing a great multitude coming toward Him, He said to Philip, 'Where shall we buy bread, that these may eat?' But this He said to test him, for He Himself knew what He would do." (John 6:5-6, NKJV)

Jesus was checking to see if Philip would tap into God's economy of sowing and reaping or Mammon's buy and sell economy. God's economy is all about the seed. He was contrasting the two economic systems. There are limitations to the world's economy. There was not enough bread, enough time, or enough to facilitate the impossible. Jesus was looking for someone to sow a seed because the seed would reap and multiply into more of its own kind.

So, where did the seed come from? The most unlikely of places.

There was a young boy in the crowd, probably the son of someone whose childcare situation fell through at the last minute, who had been told, "Here's a book and your favorite lunch of bread and some not-yet-stinky fish. Just sit here and be quiet." The disciples saw the boy with the loaves and fish and he gave his lunch to them. Jesus then instructed them to begin to divide up the boy's

---

6   Matthew 14:16

lunch and feed it to the crowd of thousands.

Wait. What?!

And the disciples trusted Him.

The disciples got back behind the microphone and told everyone of the change of plans. They started passing the loaves and fishes down the aisles and everyone took as much as they wanted. I imagine there was some grumbling about this. Taking as much as you want was not what the disciples had in mind. But after everyone had eaten, something miraculous came into view. There were 12 baskets of food left over![7]

What the boy thought was only bread was actually seed provided by God. The disciples brought the boy's lunch to Jesus and the gift was multiplied back to them – with 12 baskets left over. I believe the extra was returned to the boy.

The seed was sown. And it MULTIPLIED. What the boy saw as bread, Jesus saw as seed. The boy sowed the seed and it was multiplied.

Remember: God gives the seed and, when it is sown, He is the one who multiplies it. He doesn't require you to generate the seed nor does He request that you take responsibility for the abundant harvest. You are the sower, not the seed maker or the market maker who multiples the seed.

And then there's Barnabas.

Barnabas Sells Some Land

Remember Ananias and Sapphira? Consider them a cautionary tale. Like them, Barnabas also had a field to sell. But unlike them, when Barnabas sold his land on the island of Cyprus he laid it at the Apostles' feet. It doesn't say anywhere that this was asked

---
[7] Mark 6:34-44, John 6:1-14

of him – he just gave it out of generosity and joy. The immediate impact of sowing this money is that it met the needs of the people where it was sown. It was used to feed and clothe the people in his community and advance the ministry of the Apostles.

The impact was far-reaching and unlocked something spiritual, too. Later, Barnabas was with Paul praying and fasting with some other leaders in Antioch and the Holy Spirit spoke to them:

"As they ministered to the Lord and fasted, the Holy Spirit said, 'Now separate to Me Barnabas and Saul for the work to which I have called them.' Then, having fasted and prayed, and laid hands on them, they sent them away. So, being sent out by the Holy Spirit, they went down to Seleucia, and from there they sailed to Cyprus." (Acts 13:2-4, NKJV)

It is interesting to note that Barnabas and Paul were the first people to be commissioned by the Holy Spirit for an apostolic assignment since the ascension of Jesus. Barnabas's sowing of natural money unlocked a spiritual door as well. After Barnabas laid his financial seed at the Apostles' feet, the Holy Spirit commissioned him into his assignment. His giving unlocked his assignment. It opened the door for the message of Christ to go to the Island of Cyprus, the very place the seed came from that Barnabas laid at the Apostles feet. As a result, the Senator of Cyprus believed in Jesus and welcomed the message to the island.[8]

In other words, Barnabas was faithful with his money and he was entrusted with the true riches – his Kingdom assignment and souls.[9] Remember that money is spiritual as much as it is physical. When it is sown, it multiplies not just physically but also spiritually. When Barnabas sowed his seed, God multiplied it financially but also multiplied the number of believers in Cyprus, the very place where the seed was sown.

---

8 Acts 13:12
9 Luke 16:11

Up to this day, Cyprus is the area where the gospel is translated into multiple languages and sent through media to the Middle East and Asia via satellite. Barnabas's financial seed is still producing an unprecedented harvest of souls 2000 years after his death. He certainly invested his treasure in a heavenly account for a much more favorable return. For all eternity, Barnabas will be welcomed into the eternal homes of new friends because of his wise financial investment into the economy of the Kingdom. [10]

The seed was sown. And it MULTIPLIED.[11] It is still multiplying today. The seed for your future is in your hands.

Reaping an Abundant Harvest: Remember Abraham?

The principle of sowing and reaping is much larger in scope than just finances. The time had come for God to multiply the natural and spiritual descendants of Abraham. God requested the perfect seed—Isaac, the only promised son of Abraham, the son he waited 25 years to be born. Abraham brought his son, Isaac, up the mountain to be offered as a sacrifice. He was sowing a seed out of obedience. God did not ask for Abraham's first son Ishmael born of Hagar, but rather Isaac the promised child born of Sarah. God waited until it was completely impossible for them to have children and then he visited them and enabled them to miraculously give birth to Isaac. God supernaturally provided the seed that He would later ask Abraham to sow. God always provides the seed to the sower.

Abraham obeyed and went to "sow" his seed, his son Isaac. Before he could put the knife to Isaac, the Angel of the Lord stopped Abraham and provided a lamb instead. Since the Kingdom works with sowing and reaping instead of buying and selling, when Abraham was willing to sow his most precious seed the multiplication was explosive. And God said similarly,

---
10 Luke 16:9
11 Acts 4:32-36, 13:1-42

"I will sow my most precious seed—Jesus the Lamb of God—and the multiplication would be the salvation of all mankind."

Today every person that is born again is also a spiritual child of faithful Abraham. This seed was multiplied into countless descendants, creating financial wealth and salvation into the future. Abraham is still reaping the multiplication of the seed sown.

Abraham believed God would provide. And because of this God guaranteed His promise with an oath, with us in mind:

Then the Angel of the Lord called to Abraham a second time out of heaven, and said: "By Myself I have sworn, says the Lord, because you have done this thing, and have not withheld your son, your only son— blessing I will bless you, and multiplying I will multiply your descendants as the stars of the heaven and as the sand which is on the seashore; and your descendants shall possess the gate of their enemies. In your seed all the nations of the earth shall be blessed, because you have obeyed My voice." (Genesis 22:15-18, NKJV)

God did the same thing with Jesus. He took His most precious seed, the Word, and sowed Him into the earth. So explosive was the growth that it has the potential to save literally all of mankind.

"For it was fitting for Him, for whom are all things and by whom are all things, in bringing many sons to glory, to make the captain of their salvation perfect through sufferings." (Hebrews 2:10, NKJV)

Throughout the Bible we are given examples of how God's economy works within the regular economy. It uses real people, literal food, actual seeds and measurable wealth. It operates in the regular economy but is not of it, and will continue to do so while the earth remains. Before Abraham, God made this promise to Noah, of animal and ark fame:

"As long as the earth remains, there will be planting and

harvest, cold and heat, summer and winter, day and night."
(Genesis 8:22, NLT)

IS GOD'S BANKING SYSTEM A WISE INVESTMENT?

Remember when we mentioned that not only do we need a good vision, but we need a perfect one? The same carries through to the economy to carry out that vision. We know that God's economy is one of tithe, seed, and bread. It's a return on investment economy. Since it operates within the regular economy, let's bring back Buffett's investment principles, ones that operate within the regular economy, and apply them here.

INVEST WITHIN YOUR CIRCLE

We know that we sow our own kind. Food grows food. People produce people. Good produces good. Evil produces evil. You can't sow a pumpkin seed and get a watermelon. You can't sow a cat and get a dog. You can't sow sin and produce good and you can't put money into your Wells Fargo account and expect to reap a tennis racquet.

The seeds we sow affect not just us but also those around us, including those into the future. Similarly, the seeds others have sown before us affect us. We reap, for good and for bad, the harvest of what those before us have sown.

INVEST IN SOMETHING WITH FAVORABLE LONG-TERM PROSPECTS.

When we are investing in God's banking system, we are investing in something eternal.

"Then no one will notice that you are fasting, except your Father, who knows what you do in private. And your Father,

who sees everything, will reward you. Don't store up treasures here on earth, where moths eat them and rust destroys them, and where thieves break in and steal." (Matthew 6:18-19, NLT)*

"Don't be misled: No one makes a fool of God. What a person plants, he will harvest. The person who plants selfishness, ignoring the needs of others – ignoring God! – harvests a crop of weeds. All he'll have to show for his life is weeds! But the one who plants in response to God, letting God's Spirit do the growth work in him, harvests a crop of real life, eternal life." (Galatians 6:7-8, MSG)*

We are reaping what has been sown by others. And others in the future will reap what has been sown by us.

INVEST IN TRUSTWORTHY MANAGEMENT: REPUTATION IS YOUR MOST IMPORTANT ASSET.

God's vision is to establish the Abrahamic Covenant. He has confirmed this Covenant many times through people like Isaac, Jacob, and King David. In the person of Jesus Christ, he confirmed Himself to be trustworthy and the source of all of our hope. We have every reason to believe that this Covenant, which continues to be confirmed across thousands of years, will be fulfilled.

"God has given both his promise an his oath. These two things are unchangeable because it is impossible for God to lie. Therefore, we who have fled to him for refuge can have great confidence as we hold to the hope that lies before us. This hope is a strong and trustworthy anchor for our souls." (Hebrews 6:18-19, NLT)

God is a trustworthy anchor for our souls. In other words, His management is good. It can be counted on.

INVEST IN THAT WHICH HOLDS INTRINSIC VALUE AND A MARGIN OF SAFETY.

A tiny lunch was multiplied with 12 baskets left over. An old father untied a young boy from a sacrificial altar, and the boy went on to multiply his descendants until they could no longer be counted.

Jesus tells a parable – a story that is meant to teach a spiritual lesson – in the Gospel of Matthew. It's about a mustard seed that grows into a mighty tree just by being planted. If you have ever seen a mustard seed, you know they are tiny.

"The Kingdom of Heaven is like a mustard seed planted in a field. It is the smallest of all seeds, but it becomes the largest of garden plants; it grows into a tree, and birds come and make nests in its branches." (Matthew 13:31-32, NLT)

God uses tangible, real-world things like seeds and bread in His economy. And the seed – when sown—always multiplies.

TWO BOYS, TWO FISH, AND TWO PACKS OF JUICY FRUIT

Warren Buffett took one package of gum and turned it into two. He grew those 10 cents' worth of gum into $100 before his twelfth birthday and on and on he went, all because he knew how to operate within an economy he valued and understood.

Another young boy gave two fish and some bread to a group of overworked disciples frantic to feed a crowd. His seed multiplied so much that the disciples were left scratching their heads, wondering what to do with the leftovers.

Barnabas sold a prime piece of island real estate and out of the joy of his heart and his singular focus on spreading the gospel he eagerly gave the money away. It wasn't coerced from him. No one had to beg for it and yet it multiplied into not just providing for believers in need but also into souls for the Kingdom.

Abraham offered his own son as a sacrifice and because of his willingness to sow that most valuable seed offering, the multiplication exploded. It continues, in the form of descendants, land, and generational wealth to this day.

God's word is the ultimate seed – when sown it always multiplies. Always. It's a return on an investment that's hard to refuse. And it means God's economy, just like His vision, is perfect.

The Sower Leads Us

The prophet Isaiah beautifully sums up the seed and the grace of sowing it.

The rain and snow come down from the heavens and stay on the ground to water the earth. They cause the grain to grow, producing seed for the farmer and bread for the hungry. It is the same with my word.

I will send it out and it always produces fruit.

It will accomplish all I want it to,

And it will prosper everywhere I send it.

And you will live in joy and peace.[12]

Amen.

---

12 Isaiah 55:10-12

CHAPTER 7

THE SOLOMON EFFECT:
ROYAL GENEROSITY

"Knowledge comes, but wisdom lingers."
Calvin Coolidge

Remember how adults seemed so wise when we were kids?

Dad: If you make that face, it will freeze that way.

Mom: Don't swallow your gum or it will stay in your stomach for seven years.

Teacher: Don't put off until tomorrow what you can do today.

Grandmother: If your ear hurts with your finger in it, then take your finger out of your ear.

Pop culture and social media have been full of contemporary wisdom, too.

Hollywood: Every story can be told in two hours or less.

Jimi Hendrix: Knowledge speaks, but wisdom listens.

Twitter: Talk first. Think later.

Socrates said that the unexamined life is not worth living, though Plato would later take credit for those words. And the images we conjure of the wise sometimes look like Plato, Aristotle, and The Thinker statue looming over the Rodin Museum in Paris. Like the statues, the people they represent and the wisdom they imply feels static and stuck in time.

But wisdom doesn't sit still. And though it probably would tell you to take your finger out of your ear if it hurts, it rarely would advise you to talk first and think later.

We are all familiar with the concept of wisdom. But what is it exactly? In homage to our age of quick blogosphere facts designed to help everyone live better in a hurry, here's what a bullet-pointed blog post about wisdom might look like:

10 Things Wise People Do

Wise people use good judgment. They think through the consequences, both good and bad, of their choices.

1. Wise people are critical thinkers. Common understanding is that information + time = wisdom. But it's more than that, otherwise every person over the age of 50 playing Trivial Pursuit would be considered wise. And we all know middle-aged know-it-alls who are anything but wise.

2. Wise people have empathy, the ability to see people and situations from multiple vantage points. A wise person is adept at knowing the insides of things because they have put a priority on deep understanding.

3. Wise people are patient. Deep understanding takes persistence and intentionality.

4. Wise people think before they speak. Wisdom is about training your mind and controlling your emotions.

5. Wise people are ready. They realize the right time may be right now rather that "someday."

6. Wise people are discerning. They don't accept something just

because it is said to them. I think we can all agree that much of social media – or much of media in general – would benefit from a heavy dose of wisdom.

7. Wise people are self-aware. Do you know about the lenses through which you look? Do you acknowledge your own filters and bias? Do you know what you don't know?

8. Wise people are other-aware. They know the motivation behind others' actions and others' attitudes. They always seem like they've been studying situations and people all along.

9. Wise people admit their mistakes. They see setbacks as a learning opportunity. They are teachable.

10. Wise people are trustworthy. They make the most of their relationships.

I don't know about you, but I am drawn to people who exhibit all of these wise attributes. They have the skills to make their way through life and they are certainly the ones I'd want helping me manage my business and money. There is nothing wrong with a "10 Things" list like this. However, there's a more powerful source of wisdom and that is God's wisdom. God not only provides the tithe for you to return to Him, the seed for you to sow into His vision, and the bread to take care of your daily needs, God also supplies you with the wisdom to steward money into alignment with His vision.

So how do others gain wisdom? And how do we? Is this common formula really true?

Experience + Time = Wisdom

Partly. While it isn't wholly sufficient to define wisdom as experience over time, there is still some truth to this. As new information spreads it becomes common knowledge. In some ways the generation after us will naturally be smarter than we are. Thirty years ago the kids who knew how to use computers were considered rare geniuses, and we all turned to them when we needed to print from an MS DOS prompt. But our grandparents know how to print from their iPhones now. So common knowledge is something.

Wisdom must also be passed down intentionally. Wisdom is tested through life changes – even the traumatic ones. And the wisdom applied from these experiences needs to be passed down, on purpose, to the next generation.

Wisdom and wealth are inseparable.

Wisdom is important and to be wise we need to share with one another. But why, in a book about economy, are we talking about wisdom in the first place?

The truth of God's economy is that wisdom and wealth fit like a hand in a glove. How do we know how to differentiate what is part of God's economy and what isn't? Wisdom. Out of what God provides, how do we know what is seed and what is bread? We ask for wisdom to know which is which.

Wisdom and wealth are inseparable.

If you do not find yourself to be wise, the good news is that you can access wisdom and learn to use it. The Bible is a surprising treasure trove, so to speak, on how to manage money. It is equally as fortified with thoughts and directives on wisdom, including how wisdom relates to our money.

The Bible is one of the ways wisdom has been passed down to us. Below is a three-part take on the value of wisdom, the source of wisdom, and the reason wealth can't happen without it.

1. Finding Treasure: The Value of Wisdom

Consider this:

"For wisdom is far more valuable than rubies. Nothing you desire can compare with it." (Proverbs 8:11, NLT)

and

"They are more desirable than gold, yes than much fine gold." (Psalm 19:10, NASB)

Wisdom is better than jewels and nothing that is desirable can compare with it. Nothing that's desirable. What do you desire? That probably covers a wide range of things.

Wisdom is so valuable that money can't buy it. We know that money is temporary – it's always changing hands. It all belongs to God and God wishes for us to steward it, but money doesn't bring security. It certainly can't buy wisdom.

The prophet, Job, asked where we could find wisdom and he concluded, "It cannot be bought with gold. It cannot be purchased with silver."[1]

In other words, we can look under every rock, in every ocean, in the eyes of every animal on the earth and in every retail store at the mall, and we won't find it there. It is that rare. That precious. That valuable.

At the same time, though, wisdom is widely available to all of us, in endless measure. And although you can't buy it with money, it is somewhat paradoxically yet inextricably linked to money. Like

---

1 Job 28:15

God's economy, wisdom is not something you can buy or sell. It isn't something you lend or borrow.

I wouldn't trade my wife for anything because there is no amount of money that could be exchanged for her. She is rare, precious, and no one can find her under a rock and polish her up into a coin for trade. But at the same time, my love for her is in endless supply, constantly replenishing, and available to both of us. We can't buy it at the mall.

So, if wisdom is so priceless that it cannot be bought with money and yet it is still connected to wealth, where do we get it?

2. The Fear of the Lord: The Beginning of Wisdom

Remember back to Job? Job also says this:

"And this is what he says to all humanity: The fear of the Lord is true wisdom; to forsake evil is real understanding." (Job 28:28, NLT)

The fear of the Lord is the beginning of wisdom. The fear of the Lord is a weighty reverence for God and a tangible awareness of His goodness. When the fear of the Lord manifests in your heart, you cannot sin. Sin runs from you in the presence of the Fear of the Lord you immediately obey with joy even when you think it doesn't make sense. Solomon echoes the same truth about wisdom in his ancient writings:

"The fear of the Lord is the beginning of wisdom, And the knowledge of the Holy One is understanding." (Proverbs 9:10 NKJV)

The fear of the Lord is the perfect environment for wisdom to germinate and thrive in your life. It means that you have respect for God as the only one worthy TO fear, but also as the only one with enough power and love to enable you to cast OUT fear.[2]

---

2   1 John 4:18

The fear of the Lord means that you are listening to God's voice and not man's voice. You are aligning, with all your heart, with God's vision.

In the Old Testament, we find a prophet named Samuel. Samuel had the distinction of anointing the first two kings of Israel: Saul (who, for the record, turned out to be not such a good choice) and David, who would be the direct line through whom Jesus would later come. Before he started appointing kings, though, Samuel worked for Eli, one of the high priests of Israel.

Eli and his sons had devolved into wicked behavior and because of this they could no longer hear God's voice. So, God called 11-year-old Samuel to keep Israel together.[3] And because Samuel feared God, God could bypass the intercessory powers and talk directly to an 11-year-old.

There comes a time when you hear the voice of the Lord not just through someone else like a pastor or, in Samuel's case, a priest. You begin to hear the voice directly because we are sons and daughters, kings and priests. This doesn't mean you disregard the wisdom of others, like leaders and pastors, it means you are additionally granted direct access to God's voice.

In the time and season we are living in God is speaking differently than He ever has before. Things may not seem like they always have. We may not have a blueprint and we may worry when we don't. The truth is experiencing the fear of the Lord is the beginning of wisdom. It isn't something we DO but rather something that comes on us. We experience the fear of the Lord as His goodness and receive absolute clarity.

We know that the fear of the Lord is the beginning of wisdom. And we know that wisdom is invaluable. But why do we need it? If we are focusing on money and finance here, does wisdom play an important role there, too? Yes, and here is why.

---

3 I Samuel 3

Wisdom comes first. We search for wisdom, not wealth. We sow seed and God creates a "seed factory." We harvest, replant and reinvest, and God creates 100 "seed factories"—that is the process. We search for wisdom first because how we operate within God's economy in practical everyday life requires wisdom. It requires wisdom to recognize seed from bread and good soil from bad.

3. Prosperous Partners: Wisdom and Wealth

This is the secret to the truth of God's economy. Wisdom and wealth are twin promises. How do they work together and why would they need to go hand-in-hand? We will talk about the Biblical specifics in a moment, but here are some real-world reasons why this partnership is important:

Relationships. As you begin to prosper it will attract people. Money has the tendency to bring new "friends" out of the woodwork and this goes for both personal and professional relationships. The Bible talks about how every man with wealth has friends and the generous, wealthy man even more.[4] We like the company of people with money. We need wisdom to steward God's wealth and to discern who are the people sharing God's vision – and who aren't.

Need. We've already talked quite a bit about trusting in the wrong things, so we know that desiring wealth can bring a false sense of security in anything besides God, the provider of the seed. It can make us secure in ourselves, our job, and our ability to meet our own needs. We need wisdom to constantly be rechanneled back to God's vision: The one that says HE will provide our needs. We are stewards and sowers, not consumers and hoarders.

Voice. Sometimes the wise who are poor are quickly tuned to the sound of God's voice because they have nothing to lose in their poverty and everything to gain with their wisdom. The unwise

---

4 Proverbs 19

who are rich have everything to lose in their wealth and nothing to gain without wisdom to lead them. They are more tuned to the sound of their own voice than anyone else's because they're dependent on themselves for their own needs.

But we are not called to be either the wise poor or the foolish rich. As our wealth continues to grow, we have an even greater need for the wisdom of God in order to listen to God's voice rather than our own.

Vocation. Wisdom helps us to earn money honestly. We cannot make it through immoral means and say, "Now this belongs to God." It doesn't work that way.

Charity. Wisdom helps us not just to make money honestly, but also to give money well. If you're trying to assuage your conscience by giving away a portion of dishonestly earned money, or giving in a way that is against the character of God, that's a good indication that you are giving in the wrong way. How do we know? We ask for wisdom. A benevolent end does not justify a sinful means.

We are stewards and sowers, not consumers and hoarders.

So wisdom is invaluable. It is found in the fear of the Lord, in aligning with His vision. And we know that wisdom is the hand inside the glove of those who are thriving in Christ.[5] So let's look at this practically. How does the relationship between wisdom and wealth really work? I set out looking for a historic, real-world example and I found just the guy.

Meet Solomon.

---

5 I Corinthians 1:30

SOLOMON: STORIES FROM A WISE GUY

What if we knew the wealthiest guy there was? And what if, after showing up to his house for dinner, we also discovered him to be the wisest guy around? We'd probably want to meet him. To listen to him. To emulate him. Thankfully, not only can we listen to him and emulate him, we have many, many accounts of how to connect wisdom and wealth written by, and about, Solomon himself.

We know that God's economy is a sowing and reaping economy. And we know that when we learn to operate in that economy we are promised to reap in abundance; free of fear, full of grace, and overflowing with blessing even during the most difficult of times. There is a pattern in scripture that when we tithe we learn to reverently fear God.[6] We experience this fear of God coming upon us as the goodness of God and through it we begin to gain the wisdom of Solomon. Subsequent to such wisdom are wealth and the Glory of God.[7]

We now know, too, that like Solomon we all need wisdom when it comes to managing, talking about, and living with money.

How do we know what to do, though? Do we watch the world markets with happy trigger fingers? Do we listen to financial podcasts and meet with wealth advisors and wring our hands? Surely there must be a better way.

Fortunately, there is.

BUILDING THE HOUSE OF GOD

Solomon lived during the tenth Century BC. He was the son of David, the David of slingshot and Goliath fame, and Bathsheba, infamous for her beauty and love of bathing in the great outdoors.

---

6   Deuteronomy 14:23
7   Luke 16:11

Solomon also had some older brothers who were set to inherit the throne of their father, King David. However, God had already spoken to David and told him that Solomon would be king. So sure enough, when it came time to hand someone the scepter, lo and behold, Solomon was named the next king.

David had a love for God's house. Before Solomon was born, God named him as the next king and the one who would be responsible to build His house.

"But you will have a son who will be a man of peace and rest, and I will give him rest from all his enemies on every side. His name will be Solomon, and I will grant Israel peace and quiet during his reign. He is the one who will build a house for my Name. He will be my son and I will be his father. And I will establish the throne of his kingdom over Israel forever. Now, my son, the Lord be with you, and may you have success and build the house of the Lord your God, as he said you would." (I Chronicles 22:9-11, NIV)

Solomon proved to be an auspicious successor to the throne. He quickly became very wealthy and very powerful.

Remember how we talked about how money has a voice that is both physical and spiritual, and that it calls out to God? Solomon offered a thousand sacrifices to God and these offerings spoke, and God heard them.[8] Imagine a thousand offerings in one day, from dawn to dusk, all in pursuit of something much more important than money. He was seeking the God's help to lead His people righteously. Every offering was testifying in heaven before God's throne carrying the heartbeat of Solomon along with it. In response, God Himself appeared to him in a dream.

He said Solomon, "Ask what I shall give you!"

What a question to be asked by God!

Solomon answered with all his heart:

---

[8] I Kings 3:4

"Now, O Lord my God, you have made me king instead of my father, David, but I am like a little child who doesn't know his way around. And here I am in the midst of your own chosen people, a nation so great and numerous they cannot be counted! Give me an understanding heart so that I can govern your people well and know the difference between right and wrong. For who by himself is able to govern this great people of yours?" (I Kings 3:7-9, NLT)

Solomon was asking for wisdom. And how do you think God responded to this request? Well, He was pleased—to say the least.

"The Lord was pleased that Solomon had asked for wisdom. So God replied, "Because you have asked for wisdom in governing my people with justice and have not asked for long life or wealth or the death of your enemies – I will give you what you asked for! I will give you a wise understanding heart such as no one else has had or ever will have!

And also:

"I will give you what you did not ask for – riches and fame! No other king in all the world will be compared to you for the rest of your life!" (I Kings 3:10-13, NLT)

With this unbelievable promise in hand, Solomon went on to build the first Jewish temple in Jerusalem. It took twenty years to build and was dedicated to the God of Israel, along with the palace that was Solomon's home. It was also home to the Ark of the Covenant. David had been instructed by God to hand the temple-building job off to Solomon, and he gave Solomon an offering. So Solomon had no small amount of building materials to work with:

"I have worked hard to provide materials for building the Temple of the Lord – nearly 4000 tons of gold, 40,000 tons of silver, and so much iron and bronze that it cannot be weighed. I have also gathered timber and stone for the walls, though you may need to add more. You have a large number of skilled

stonemasons and carpenters and craftsmen of every kin. You have expert goldsmiths and silversmiths and workers of bronze and iron. Now begin the work, and may the Lord be with you." (1 Chronicles 22:14-16, NLT)

In addition, David gave from his personal account a total of 112 tons of gold and 262 tons of silver. His leaders gave an additional 108 tons of gold and ten thousand gold coins. [9]

For some perspective, in today's money USD:

- This 4000 tons of gold would be valued at approximately 164 billion dollars.

- The 40,000 tons of silver would be worth about 20 billion dollars.

- David's 112 tons of gold would be valued today at 4.5 billion dollars.

- David's 262 tons of silver is now approximately 6 million dollars.

- The 188 tons of gold from his leaders of tribes would be 7.7 billion dollars.

This does not include the stone, wood, jewels and other materials, or the labor it took to build it. This does not include the value of the land either. Just the materials alone in today's money would be worth well over $200 billion USD. By comparison to something we can tangibly see and experience today, the Vatican is worth about $15 billion dollars total.[10] In other words, the temple was to a scale none of us have ever seen.

The temple made a bit of a splash in the community. Just as God had promised, Solomon's wealth became famous. And Solomon's God became famous, as well.

God made Solomon so wise and wealthy that even other powerful rulers, such as the Queen of Sheba, wanted to meet

---

9 1 Chronicles 29:4-7
10 All values were correct at the time of writing.

him. "This guy, Solomon overflows with God's wisdom, owns all kinds of stuff, and knows all kinds of important people," the queen probably thought. "It's time I go introduce myself to him." So she did.[11]

Road Trip: A Curious Queen Meets A Wise King

The Queen of Sheba was famous in ancient times. The Jews told stories about her and ancient historians like Josephus wrote about her. Artists have captured her for centuries. She was kind of a big deal. So naturally, the fact that she wanted to meet Solomon was kind of a big deal, too.

Meeting day started as per usual for the royals. She arrived in Jerusalem with a large group of attendants, a caravan of camels loaded with spices, and a substantial cache of gold and jewels. But when she arrived, the reality of Solomon's wealth superseded even the rumors. He was indeed very, very rich. His palace had extravagant food on every table, fabulous clothing, servants at every turn, more jewels than she could look at in a day and on and on it went. In fact, the queen herself described it as overwhelming. It would have been like Bill Gates showing up and saying, "Oh, so this is how rich people live!"

The queen came out of honor and curiosity. She arrived with a bunch of questions prepared for Solomon. But Solomon had answers for all of her questions; nothing was too hard for the king to explain to her.

"Everything that I heard about you while still in my country was true," she said.[12]

She didn't believe it until she saw it with her own eyes and heard it with her own ears. And before she left Solomon (with departing

---

11 I Kings 10:1-2
12 I Kings 10:6

gifts of 9000 pounds of gold, precious jewels, and spices), she said something interesting about Solomon's wealth, and about the wisdom connected to it.

"I didn't believe what was said until I arrived here and saw it with my own eyes. In fact, I had not heard the half of it! Your wisdom and prosperity are far beyond what I was told. 8 How happy your people must be! What a privilege for your officials to stand here day after day, listening to your wisdom! 9 Praise the Lord your God, who delights in you and has placed you on the throne of Israel. Because of the Lord's eternal love for Israel, he has made you king so you can rule with justice and righteousness." (I Kings 10:7-9, NLT)

Writing Wisdom

So Solomon became wise because he asked to be wise. But how'd he get so wealthy? The queen seems to think they were inseparably related and she was right. God promised that wealth would follow wisdom.

And when wealth followed wisdom just as He had promised, Solomon went on to write all about it.

Solomon, in addition to expanding his armies and building a temple, collected and penned some of our most beloved ancient texts. One of those is a collection of 31 essays, poems and other writings that, both in his time and ours, hold up as words to live by. There's even a bit of satire thrown in for good measure.

This collection is a part of the Old Testament called Proverbs. Proverbs is a wide-ranging book that discusses, among other things, values, morals, and the overall human condition. It set the stage for what would continue for the next several millennia as something of a wisdom tradition.

Solomon seems to be the expert both at being wise and being rich, and Proverbs seems to be the place that he writes about them and the way that wisdom is handed down to us. So what, then, does Proverbs have to say about wisdom and its relationship to wealth?

Fortunately for us: a lot.

PROVERBS: GUIDEBOOK TO WISDOM

The Book of Proverbs means, literally, a book of comparisons and contrasts.[13] It is a collection of writings that compares and contrasts similar things. As I mentioned above, Solomon is responsible for writing or collecting writing for most of the Proverbs. He delivers the purpose of the book to us succinctly, thesis-style, right at the beginning:

"Their purpose is to teach people wisdom and discipline, to help them understand the insights of the wise. Their purpose is to teach people to live disciplined and successful lives, to help them do what is right, just and fair. These proverbs will give insight to the simple, knowledge and discernment to the young." (Proverbs 1:2-4, NLT)

Solomon goes on to encourage us to:

"Let the wise listen to these proverbs and become even wiser." (v 5)

Fortunately wisdom, it seems, has no end to its usefulness or availability.

THE LIVING WORD: WISDOM CONSTANTLY REPLENISHES

We have talked about wise investing and sticking with what has good and lasting value. As investments go, wisdom is the best

---

13 Malick, D. An Introduction to the Book of Proverbs. Bible.org. Taken from: https://bible.org/article/introduction-book-proverbs

one. Gold used to be the standard for most earthly economies; however, God's economy is based on a higher standard:

"Choose my instruction rather than silver, and knowledge rather than pure gold. For wisdom is far more valuable than rubies. Nothing you desire can compare with it." (Proverbs 8:10-11, NLT)

This is a pretty big statement from the wealthiest guy in the land. Yes, the money is important. And yes, God uses wealth to fulfill the Covenant and further His vision. But wisdom is the hand holding the gold and the rubies. It is a seed that, when planted, multiplies endlessly. Jesus is an example of this.

Paul's first letter to the church at Corinth describes Jesus, the ultimate example of the multiplied seed, as the one "who became for us wisdom from God—and righteousness and sanctification and redemption."[14]

You can receive knowledge from Proverbs continuously – and in new ways – because these most valuable writings were birthed through wisdom. The Wisdom of God will reveal the future. And you can read them over and over again and receive new revelation each time.

In verse 15, wisdom continues to define herself in some pretty hefty ways.

"Common sense and success belong to me. Insight and strength are mine. Because of me, kings reign, and rulers make just decrees."

By asking for wisdom, Solomon, the wealthiest king, was able to rule a kingdom. Likewise, if we seek God and His wisdom diligently, we will receive it. We rule and reign by Him, through His wisdom.

---

[14] I Corinthians 1:30

The Queen of Sheba didn't just notice Solomon's wisdom and palace, though that was certainly what drew her to him in the first place. She took note that even his servants were happy, that everyone around him, at every level, seemed to have a special spirit about them. You and I have access to that same Spirit through wisdom.

God supplies the Spirit of Wisdom. Wisdom constantly replenishes and consistently multiplies. It affects, but also reflects, the sowing and reaping bedrock of God's economy. The Bible references three kinds of wisdom: human wisdom, demonic wisdom and God's Wisdom. The latter is what you are looking for and the first two are just poor substitutes.[15]

These three kinds of wisdom are defined by the source from which they originate.

HUMAN WISDOM

The source of human wisdom is the soul (mind, will, emotions) of a person and is rooted in the world's way of thinking. It is based on the physical and intellectual realm of human reasoning devoid of inspiration. Within the early New Testament church, they struggled to wrap their minds around God's concept of Wisdom. The Apostle Paul in his first letter to the Corinthians, contrasts human wisdom and God's wisdom this way:

"I will destroy the wisdom of the wise and discard the intelligence of the intelligent." So where does this leave the philosophers, the scholars, and the world's brilliant debaters? God has made the wisdom of this world look foolish. Since God in his wisdom saw to it that the world would never know him through human wisdom, he has used our foolish preaching to save those who believe." (1 Corinthians 1:19-21, NLT)

---

15 1 Corinthians 1:17

I will destroy the wisdom of the wise, God said. This means His wisdom is far superior to human wisdom. It crushes human wisdom and reveals its folly. The wisest person on earth doesn't even come close to God's Wisdom. His Wisdom is so far superior to ours that it stands out. Paul expounds further about and continues to contrast God's wisdom:

"It is foolish to the Jews, who ask for signs from heaven. And it is foolish to the Greeks, who seek human wisdom. So when we preach that Christ was crucified, the Jews are offended and the Gentiles say it's all nonsense. But to those called by God to salvation, both Jews and Gentiles, Christ is the power of God and the wisdom of God. This foolish plan of God is wiser than the wisest of human plans, and God's weakness is stronger than the greatest of human strength." (1 Corinthians 1:22-25, NLT)

THE BIBLE REFERENCES THREE KINDS OF WISDOM: HUMAN WISDOM, DEMONIC WISDOM AND GOD'S WISDOM.

Note human wisdom does not lead one to know God, but the fruit of God's wisdom is a revelation of the source of wisdom—Christ the wisdom and power of God.

In the same letter Paul explains that this type of human wisdom makes the work that Jesus accomplished on the cross ineffective in the life of a person.[16]

However, this does not mean that if someone does not believe in or know God that everything they say is automatically human wisdom. They may have learned a wisdom principle from someone else, not realizing it was God's wisdom, and successfully adopted it in their own life. Then they pass on that wisdom principle to generations that follow. Oblivious to its source, it still benefits

---
16 1 Corinthians 1:17

the hearer. God's wisdom is ageless in its application and pure in its origin.

DEMONIC WISDOM

This wisdom is sourced in invisible entities in the unseen realm that have influenced and continue to influence mankind through various means. This wisdom is often darkness cloaked as light. It may even appear noble, but the intent is always destructive. This next Biblical text describes a few symptoms of demonic wisdom.

"But if you are bitterly jealous and there is selfish ambition in your heart, don't cover up the truth with boasting and lying. For jealousy and selfishness are not God's kind of wisdom. Such things are earthly, unspiritual, and demonic. For wherever there is jealousy and selfish ambition, there you will find disorder and evil of every kind." (James 3:14-16, NLT)

> **GOD'S WISDOM CHALLENGES OUR MINDSETS, ELEVATES OUR THINKING AND CHANGES OUR PERSPECTIVE.**

Jealousy, bitterness, and selfish-ambition are all rooted in demonic wisdom and lead to confusion, disorder, and evil. These attitudes are designed to distract our focus and corrupt our hearts with hatred and blind us to what is important. Demonic wisdom can ruin a family, corrupt a government, and incite war to destroy nations. Tyranny and oppression of mankind is rooted in demonic wisdom and in the motives of jealousy, bitterness and selfish ambition. What does this all have to do with a book about money? Well, God's wisdom tells us that the love of money is the root of all kinds of evil.[17] Notice not money, but the love of it. Demonic wisdom functions through the love of money and is a hallmark of Mammon's economy. It's important to note when we

---

17 I Timothy 6:10

love, trust and pursue money demonic wisdom finds expression through our lives. This leads to no good end.

By contrast, God's wisdom:

"But the wisdom from above is first of all pure. It is also peace loving, gentle at all times, and willing to yield to others. It is full of mercy and the fruit of good deeds. It shows no favoritism and is always sincere." (James 3:17, NLT)

GOD'S WISDOM

God's wisdom is strategic and applicable in our personal lives and is His primary battle strategy to help us fulfill His vision. His wisdom sees every angle and knows the future, the beginning and the end. Here is more insight from Paul's letter to the Ephesians:

"God's purpose in all this was to use the church to display his wisdom in its rich variety to all the UNSEEN rulers and authorities in the heavenly places." (Ephesians 3:10, NLT)[18]

The aim of God's wisdom is to deploy His battle strategy through you against the unseen, invisible rulers operating behind the scenes affecting our world. Have you ever wondered what is wrong with our world? These unseen demonic entities are deceitful and use people to express their ideas and ideologies in our world over millennia. We live in a world where concepts, ideas, and philosophies are always at odds. Some of these ideologies are sourced in demonic wisdom and mixed with human wisdom and reasoning. This combination is lethal and intersects with our everyday lives, often with us too busy to notice. These ideas and concepts affect our way of thinking and over time become mindsets that we adopt in our lives through our culture, society, and upbringing. God's wisdom challenges our mindsets, elevates our thinking, and changes our perspective.[19]

---

18 Emphasis added.
19 Romans 8:5-6

"Put on all of God's armor so that you will be able to stand firm against all strategies of the devil. For we are not fighting against flesh-and-blood enemies, but against evil rulers and authorities of the UNSEEN world, against mighty powers in this dark world, and against evil spirits in the heavenly places." (Ephesians 6:11-12, NLT[20])

Sometimes the unusual resistance and circumstances we face are symptoms of a spiritual battle, taking place over us in the unseen world. Your assignment requires God's wisdom strategies to counteract the obstacles in your path and the demonic strategies at work in our world. On your journey in life you have a part to play in God's redemptive vision to bless mankind. The economic strategies in this book are weapons of wisdom in your armory against the unseen forces of this world. God gives us the power and wisdom to create wealth. Understanding the purpose of wealth gives you the opportunity to align money with God's vision and benefit our world.

Wisdom is also the language, vernacular, and vocabulary of money.

In this battle, the wisdom of this world and demonic wisdom are no match for the Wisdom of God. Here is more insight from Solomon's ancient writings:

There is no [human] wisdom or understanding, or counsel [that can prevail] against the Lord. (Proverbs 21:30, AMP)

In our complicated world there is a confrontation of ideas and resulting actions often motivated by masters in the unseen spirit world. God wants to put His wisdom on display through your life to these puppeteers in the unseen world. Solomon goes on to say:

---

20 Emphasis added.

"The horse is prepared for the day of battle, but deliverance and victory belong to the Lord. (Proverbs 21:31 AMP)

God's wisdom brings victory to the initiatives of your life.

His wisdom is spiritual and practical and superior to both worldly and demonic wisdom. Wisdom is valuable, self-sustaining, and game-changing. Wisdom is also the language, vernacular, and vocabulary of money. Those considered wisest in Mammon's economy are not in God's.[21] God adds a layer of HIS wisdom that gives us grace to operate within HIS economy. God's superior system brings blessing and works well within the world's economy.

Remember Warren Buffett and his admonishment not to be given to greed or impulsive behavior?

We all know what it's like to buy a new car, a new pair of shoes, or a pool for our backyard only later to regretfully remember that we live in Northern Ontario, that we already have 37 pair of expensive shoes that didn't make us happy, and that we don't want to announce our midlife crisis when driving our kids to soccer practice. Proverbs says:

"The plans of the diligent lead to profit, as surely as haste leads to poverty." (Proverbs 21:5, NIV)

If we know we have a problem with impulse control, we should stay out of stores or only buy with cash. Set yourself up to be wise. And consider long-term what your investment is, then buy later. If the car or shoes or pool are really a good idea, they will still be a good idea tomorrow or next week. Wisdom would say that it isn't wrong to buy things – even expensive things – but consider them first.

---

21 I Corinthians 2:8

Wisdom Brings Influence

Speaking of expensive things, let's go back to Solomon and the Queen of Sheba.

One of the intrinsic benefits of kingship is the wisdom of God. We know wisdom was the bedrock of Solomon's kingship.

Why was there nothing that Solomon couldn't explain to the Queen of Sheba? It was because of the wisdom of God. It isn't that he wasn't smart and educated – he probably was – but it doesn't compare to the wisdom of God. It took her breath away when she saw this. The Queen had heard rumors about Solomon concerning the word of the Lord but it turned out that kingship wasn't about Solomon. Kingship is not about you, either. Kingship is about the King of Kings.

Kingship is about the King of Kings.

We are kings in the Kingdom of God. Not earthly kings like Solomon, but we are kings in God's Kingdom, which is to imply that we are not all detached rulers over our own little tiny kingdoms. Instead, the Apostle Paul says in his letter to the Church in Rome, that those who have received abundant grace and the gift righteousness have been called to reign.[22] Whether it's something small like a family or large like a city, we are called to have influence.

We serve the King of Kings and we are called to rule by having power over the evil forces in this world. But we are also here to develop and express our kingly—priestly nature. We posture our lives so God can serve others through us. We function as kingly

---

[22] Romans 5:17

servants and royal priests. Jesus is the ultimate example of a humble king. We are learning how to be faithful with little so we can be entrusted with much.

And in both cases, wisdom is required for us to operate in our kingship. God's wisdom is released through the Spirit of God and His Word. Wisdom not only precedes wealth, but also precedes the holy throne of God.

When Solomon inherited money, he prayed and asked the Lord for wisdom. Why? So he could rightly lead God's people. Kingship is about leading people. Kingship is about surrendering to God and receiving His will. His thoughts are higher than our thoughts and His ways are higher than our ways. However, wisdom is the revelation of His thoughts and His amazing ways.

Solomon also wrote a book called Ecclesiastes. In the Old Testament, this book comes right after Proverbs and is famous for its repeated mantra, "Meaningless, meaningless, all is meaningless!" Solomon's existential crisis led him to beg God for wisdom above all else and God delivered.

"So I decided there is nothing better than to enjoy food and drink and to find satisfaction in work. Then I realized that these pleasures are from the hand of God. For who can eat or enjoy anything apart from him? God gives wisdom, knowledge and joy to those who please him. But if a sinner becomes wealthy, God takes the wealth away and gives it to those who please him. This, too, is meaningless – like chasing the wind." (Ecclesiastes 2:24-26, NLT)

In the same way that trusting in ourselves or money to meet our own needs bypasses God's economy and aligns with Mammon's economy, Solomon is pointing out that depending on ourselves for wisdom is like chasing the wind. It's desiring, trusting and pursuing the wrong thing and, eventually, it will burn itself out. But God's wisdom is for today, tomorrow and forever.

Wisdom is married to wealth and in God's economy this infuses meaning into our lives. Existential crisis averted.

When Solomon was king, the wealth entrusted to him multiplied exponentially. But the specific numbers are not what is important here. It doesn't matter if you have ten dollars or ten million dollars. God is going to take you from where you are to the next place.

The fear of the Lord is the beginning of wisdom (Wisdom comes before wealth. Wisdom is given to us before God aligns His wealth for His glory)

Here is how Solomon describes this connection:

(Wisdom says) "I love all who love me. Those who search will surely find me. I have riches and honor, as well as enduring wealth and justice. My gifts are better than gold, even the purest gold, my wages better than sterling silver! I walk in righteousness, in paths of justice. Those who love me inherit wealth. I will fill their treasuries." (Proverbs 8:17-21, NLT)

WISDOM LINGERS

Calvin Coolidge was right. Knowledge comes, but wisdom lingers.

President Coolidge was known for his quiet demeanor. His nickname was "Silent Cal." And while we know that silence is sometimes golden and often, like the statues, considered wise, we also know that wisdom is timeless in many forms.

Solomon's message lingers.

Solomon was both wise and wealthy for one reason: Because he asked God to make him wise. We can do that, too.

Proverbs' message lingers.

Nothing can compare with God's wisdom. It is invaluable to every moment of our lives.

"There is no wisdom, no insight, no plan that can succeed against the Lord." (Proverbs 21:30, NIV)

Neither human wisdom nor demonic wisdom can succeed against the Wisdom of the Lord.

The generational wealth message lingers.

Do not fear downturns. Money isn't getting lost, it's only changing hands. This is as true now as it has ever been and wisdom is the hand helping us to thrive into our future.

And God's Covenant lingers on and on and on. We are still talking about it.

Wisdom is for all time. This is why God gives an open invitation to all to ask for wisdom:

"If any of you lacks wisdom, you should ask God, who gives generously to all without finding fault, and it will be given to you." (James 1:5, NIV)

If you ask God for wisdom He will not disappoint.

CHAPTER 8

WEATHER FORECAST:
UPTURNS, DOWNTURNS, AND A PIZZA

> *"The recipe for surviving – even thriving – in the current economy may be less tax cut extension and more bubbling cheese, savory tomato sauce and chewy crust."*
>
> John Berman

Do you love watching a storm? I do. I love watching the sky darken, the clouds gather, and the wind pick up. I don't wish for storms to be the norm, of course, but I actually look forward to them. A part of the reason is because of what I know happens as a result of the storm and what follows.

As much as I like watching the storm roll in, I more look forward to that first moment the sun cracks open the clouds. I always know that moment is coming and the promise of it is thrilling. God designed the same wind that blew in the storm to blow it back out, leaving replenished vegetation, fuller water reservoirs, and cleaner skies in its wake.

Economic storms work much the same way. You've probably seen them coming.

If you've been alive for a length of time that can be measured in decades, it's likely that you can feel when the economic climate begins to shift. Not necessarily because the news channels are promoting it but because you just sense the shift. Like any good farmer, you can look to the sky, hold up your finger, and sense impending recession blowing in on the wind.

Sometimes it's the big indicators: there's low overall economic growth, rising unemployment, falling house prices, and a generally low consumer confidence. And other times it's a series of small things strung together—the price of milk is up or gasoline prices have slowly risen over the last three weeks. You could swear there are fewer things on the shelves at your local store. And there were those two friends who casually mentioned that their kids dropped their lessons this week.

When the tops of the trees begin to sway with change that's blowing in, we say things like, "Well, we were going to take that anniversary trip to Hawaii, but we've heard the economy is about to get rough, so maybe we will wait until next year." Or "I guess we aren't going to sell our house because the inventory is going up and we need to prepare for prices to go down." Or maybe you just find yourself making the subconscious choice of store brand peanut butter over the name brand.

But when the signs of recession start sneaking up to your front door, your dinner plates and even your Hawaiian vacation, take heart. That pending recession isn't going to happen to you—it's going to happen for you.

COMES WITH EXTRA CHEESE: LESSONS FROM THE HUT

While the country stayed mired in the downturn of 2008, in 2009 Pizza Hut introduced a $10 large pizza with up to three toppings that could feed a family of four. The result: In one year, Pizza Hut's business was up 8%. They began offering two medium pizzas for 5.99 each and in the third quarter alone their sales were up 11.7%. They figured out how to easily and inexpensively (the twin hallmarks of successful recession-era businesses) deliver their product to their customers.

In fact, the pizza industry in general did well during the last recession. Like the depression-era companies who followed Walt

Disney nearly 100 years ago, some of our modern companies fell in line with Pizza Hut's lead, too.

That pending recession isn't going to happen to you—it's going to happen for you.

Bloomberg set out to study what companies did to thrive in the last recession and what they are doing to plan for flourishing in the next one.[1] Here's some of what they learned:

Make life easier. Companies who are still thriving made big deals out of the little things that made our lives easier. Alaska Airlines offered more legroom and power outlets at their weary travelers' seats. This was directly in opposition to other airlines that were trying to survive by scrapping these smaller conveniences.

Invest aggressively. We talked about Warren Buffett's strategy earlier, but it is as true today as it ever has been. With any amount of cash they have on hand, flourishing companies are buying low and waiting for the high—which always comes.

Hone systems and processes. Bloomberg points out that during a downturn thriving companies narrow the most critical components of their systems and processes. In doing this, they can bring innovative cost savings to their companies.

Lead Well. The recession-proof companies inspire, incentivize, and invest in their people. Like Henry Ford before them, modern companies that survive and thrive in economic downturns have respected, well-paid employees on their side.

---

1 Crawford, F. (2014). Bloomberg L.P. This Is What Companies That Survive Recessions Do Right. Retrieved from: https://www.bloomberg.com/news/articles/2014-08-29/the-companies-that-can-survive-recession-do-these-things-right

Commit to a clear purpose and vision. IKEA knows it and we do, too. Without a clear vision the company, the industry, and the people perish.

Notice, each of these take wisdom. In fact, they require wisdom that at the time might have sounded foolish.

RECASTING THE VISION: THE READING OF THE WILL

God is the great visionary. His vision is to:

Establish and confirm the Abrahamic Covenant, and to fulfill this by blessing all people of the world through the gospel of the Kingdom in the person of Jesus Christ.[2]

God has perfect vision. But why do we care about money in relationship to this? Because money is an integral part of God's vision. Remember this verse from the Book of Deuteronomy?[3]

"Remember the Lord your God. He is the one who gives you power to be successful, in order to fulfill the covenant he confirmed to your ancestors with an oath."

God bound Himself to His oath and this oath requires the exchange of money. This contract guaranteed land, descendants, and wealth. The Law of Due Consideration says that in order for an oath to be valid, three things have to be true: the living will must be binding, it has to be in the form of a contract rather than a gift, and an exchange of money has to take place to unlock the it.

For instance, if you wanted to gift your house to your brother, you would need to file paperwork to receive a contract of homeownership. But for the contract to be valid, you would need

---

2   Galatians 3:8, 3:17, Ephesians 2:19-22, Matthew 28:18-20
3   Deuteronomy 8:18

to sell your brother the house for $1, because it's money that binds the contract. Similarly, tithe is the Law of Due Consideration that binds us to the willed estate God has promised to us, the promise He has unilaterally bound Himself to.

In addition to money, what is the other thing needed for a will to be contractual? A death. There is no reading of the will without a death. The part of the Abrahamic Covenant that includes "The person of Jesus Christ," with whose death we are familiar, binds us to God's contract.

Since God's purpose is to re-channel wealth back into His vision, money is going to continue to change hands. Upturns and downturns must take place to re-order wealth into God's economy. This may include natural disasters, famines, and shaking the economies of all nations. But there is no need to be afraid. All of this is not happening to you, but for you! Whoever cooperates with God's vision has access to God's wealth.

These take wisdom. In fact, they require wisdom that at the time might have sounded foolish.

NEW MIND, NEW HEART AND THE FEAR OF BIRDS

I have a friend who is terrified of birds. All birds. Birds in mass, like the pigeons in St. Mark's Square in Venice. Birds sitting silent and hungry, like the seagulls who try and look casual while they sideways-eye your lunch. Even a pretty bluebird is eyed with suspicion unless it is firmly statuesque on the other side of a piece of a double pane of glass.

This fear doesn't make a lot of sense. Clearly none of these birds, whether it's a few of them or a lot of them, are going to harm him. But we fear what we don't understand, what triggers our emotions; and what fuels our misplaced worry.

Similarly, with the wrong mind and heart we've tended to look at money like it's the bluebird, and then from within that fear and misunderstanding we operate as if we're in an economic Alfred Hitchcock film.

So even with a good vision in place, we need to align our hearts and minds with the truth about economy. To change your mind, you need inspiration. But you can't behave your way to a new mindset. You must change your heart.

Change your heart, change your mind.

The mindset of the new economy – God's Economy – is this:

Money is natural AND it is spiritual.

Money is not evil. It just belongs in its proper place. It's either clean or unclean. If we miss the purpose of it, it can bring corruption. But if we understand the purpose of it, it will lead us to the glory of God.

There is a rightful place where money is destined to go. We've discussed how money has a divine signature, voice, and destination. Haggai, Abel, and Cornelius testified to the movement of money to its rightful place. Their stories taught how sometimes money cries out to be re-channeled back to its destination. The woman with the alabaster box knew the right home for her expensive perfume, and her gift became a voice. The money spoke.

In this context let's look at these words of Jesus again.

"Don't store up treasures here on EARTH, where moths eat them and rust destroys them, and where thieves break in and steal. Store your treasures in HEAVEN, where moths and rust cannot destroy, and thieves do not break in and steal." (Matthew 6:19-20, NLT[4])

---
4 Emphasis added

Jesus is making it clear that investments in the world's economy are subject to inflation, theft, and corrosion and are not secure. By contrast, heaven's economy and banking system is inflation-proof, and fireproof and comes with a guaranteed return. First, notice there is a secure heavenly investment account you have access to. Second, God's big idea is for you to take unrighteous money out of this world's economy and invest it God's economy. Remember, God simply intends to transfer wealth from under Mammon's control, through our hands, into God's governance for His vision. God will give you the power to get wealth to do just that.

In addition to understanding the co-mingling of the natural and spiritual aspects of money, to have the right mindset about economy we also need to:

Divest ourselves of the lies we believe about money.

Lies like: money exclusively supplies our needs. Or, we should hate money and value poverty. Or, we are unfit or we can do better for ourselves than what God can provide for us.

Have you ever read the statistics of people who win the lottery?[5] About 70% of lottery winners will go broke or will be back where they started in five years. 70 percent! Why is this? Because they don't know the purpose of the money: why they have it and what is it for. And when we don't understand the purpose of wealth, we can't hold onto it. Yes, some people are foolish with money, but it's much more than that.

By not understanding that their physical money is also spiritual and being governed by a system attached to it, they both trust it and fear it. This is Mammon's economy. Mammon's money ensures that we trust money even though money will be shaken up and out of our hands sometimes without us realizing it—because that money has places to go and a purpose to fulfill.

---

5   Dixon, T. (2016). Why do 70 percent of lottery winner end up bankrupt? Cleveland.com. Advance Ohio. Retrieved from: http://www.cleveland.com/business/index.ssf/2016/01/why_do_70_percent_of_lottery_w.html

We need to free ourselves from the lies Mammon tells us because a bad mindset is a perfect playground for fear. The fear of being poor, of being rich, of not being enough and of the endless "what ifs" play havoc with our view of the future and understanding of the past. It is the kind of fear that winning the lottery comes packaged with: the risk of losing it all and that can keep us from the wealth available in God's economy.

But it doesn't have to come packaged with fear. God is perfect love and perfect love casts out fear. Understanding God's purpose for money makes money work for us rather than the other way around. No more fear.

> **Whoever cooperates with God's vision has access to God's wealth.**

This same perfect Love also does something else, something huge in economic terms: He promises to supply all our needs.

All of them.

THE WAR OVER WEALTH: ECONOMIC SHOWDOWN

We've learned the first two components of the new economy:

1. God's economy requires a different mindset. It is one economy operating within another in both a natural and spiritual way.

2. God's economy is perfect. It is free from moths and rust. It is recession-proof, and fireproof and is constantly replenishing. It frees us from fear and worry about money.

But to understand what else is at the heart of God's economy, there are a few additional factors. First:

3. We need to know and understand the economic gods.

Every economy is based on an economic system and each has governing bodies and structures controlling that system. We have two choices: Mammon's economy or God's economy.

Mammon's economy is a fixed-sum, fixed resources, fixed everything system that hinges on our love for, trust in, and pursuit of money. Mammon's economy looks at life with a scarcity mentality and makes us crazy in the cycle of trusting money to provide for us.

God's economy is an open sum system with unlimited resources. It looks at life as one of abundance. John 10:10 says, "I've come that you may have life and have it more abundantly." While Mammon would have us fixated on what we don't have, Jesus came to radically change that. God's economy has us fixated on Him. And in Him we have everything we will ever need.

Next, after we know and understand our economic gods, we choose to align with the vision and purpose promised by that system. Money will be necessary to fulfill that vision. In God's economy, wealth has never been outside of God's plan. However, it is not the central focus of His plan. It's just a tool.

When we understand the structure and governance of the economic system we choose, next we need to align with the subsystems and processes within that system.

Mammon's economy has us trying to endlessly meet our own needs by desiring, trusting, and pursuing money. But God has a distinctly different framework upon which His entire economy is built:

God asks us to desire, trust, and pursue Him.

This is the center of His economic system, the scaffolding holding everything together. So how do we do that? To switch to a different economic system, we need to change the object of our desire. Our needs cannot be the object of our desire. Instead:

God is the object of our desire.

And once we change the object of our desire, this changes the entire economic process.

Instead of praying for, working to, and striving for enough money to meet our own needs, we cease striving and can be at peace that God will meet our needs. Remember the birds? Not only are we not afraid of them, Jesus reminds us, we look to them for inspiration: Remember the birds and the lilies.[6]

> **MAMMON'S ECONOMY IS A FIXED-SUM, FIXED RESOURCES, FIXED EVERYTHING SYSTEM THAT HINGES ON OUR LOVE FOR, TRUST IN, AND PURSUIT OF MONEY.**

4. We move from a buy-sell economy to a sow-reap one.

Here's what happens in the sow-reap economy: Recessions become not only something we don't need to dread and fear, they become an important doorway through which we are excited to walk, an adventure we're ready to take on. Because it's during the downturns that we are reminded that recession is not fatal. Famine is not the end. In fact, we are reminded that shakings are not happening to us, but for us. They're to be enthusiastically expected because God is going to use them for us in an exciting way.

CRISIS IS THE CRADLE OF WEALTH, INNOVATION, AND INGENUITY

Remember Abraham and how economic shakings not only

---
6 Matthew 6:26

prospered him but also gave him more descendants and money than he knew what to do with? And, after Isaac sowed his seed into the dry ground, God multiplied it? Joseph was reminded that God preserves generational wealth and when there's famine it's time to MULTIPLY! I went from living in my car to prospering because I sowed the seed I had. The reason this happened in times of economic challenge rather than during times of economic prosperity is because:

5. God's economy is a seed-based system that multiplies.

It is an investment system, an exponential/multiplication system. The Bank of God is based not in gold or silver but in seed. His system relies on a releasing of tithe, sowing of seed and eating of bread. We don't have to mine for the seed like we do for gold, or worry that it is going to run out like we do our natural resources. God continuously supplies the seed and bread.

The seed will multiply when it leaves your hand and lands in God's control. It multiplies where it is sent – for God to use it, but also back to you. But just like a willed estate requires a death for it to be valid, a death is required for a seed to grow and multiply as well. The seed must die in order for it to bloom. We aren't afraid of the seed process in farming or gardening and likewise we shouldn't be afraid of it when it comes to our finances.

Sowing is the way of God. It can be about money, but it isn't just about money. Just like people copy Warren Buffett to see the same returns he does, if you operate in God's ways you will get the same results He does. Abraham sowed his son, Isaac. The little boy sowed his lunch. Sowing is deliberate and consistent. It's stewardship. With what God provides, we do three things: Release our tithe. Sow our seed. And live on our bread.

Every offering is seed. However, every seed is not an offering. An offering is an expression of worship to God. Sowing seed encompasses all aspects of giving, offerings, and generosity.

Just remember:

Don't sow your bread and you can't eat your seed.

So out of every $100 we make, $10 is returned as tithe. The remaining amount is divided between your seed and your bread.

We return our tithe back to God first. Then we sow our seed, expectantly knowing that God will multiply it. If you eat your seed you are consuming your future. Finally, we eat our bread. And how do we know which is seed and which is bread? How do we know how much to sow and how much to eat?

We ask for wisdom. Wisdom helps us discern what may at first glance look like bread but is actually seed.

SWEET TO YOUR SOUL: A KEY WORD ABOUT EVERLASTING HOPE

Rich, wise guy Solomon never asked God for money. He asked God for wisdom because wisdom is priceless. Wisdom is what comes before wealth and when we look for it we will find it in the fear of God. Wisdom helps us to use our work, our minds, and our influence for good. It is for today. It's for the future. And it is our last principle of economy:

6. Wisdom holds wealth in its hand.

Wisdom brings something extra with it, too: hope.

"In the same way, wisdom is sweet to your soul. If you find it, you will have a bright future, and your hopes will not be cut short." (Proverbs 24:14, NLT)

Money affects every day of our lives and we exchange it for what we need and want. It constantly changes hands.

In God's economy, we have a clear vision for our money. God is going to use it. He's going to use us to channel money back to His vision. This depends on us desiring only Him, trusting only Him, pursuing only Him. It means getting to the truth of economy: that downturns in the economy are a normal and welcome part of life. They are the shakings that get money back to the right hands, back to the right house, and back where it belongs. They are happening for us to help us.

IF YOU EAT YOUR SEED YOU ARE CONSUMING YOUR FUTURE.

Mammon's goal is to keep everyone serving money. But the love of money brings corruption because it aligns with a bad vision, a flawed system, and a fixed outcome.

But God's vision is perfect. Every downturn results in an upturn for His people. From famine to wealth. From fear to freedom. From foolish to wise, and from fixed to unlimited blessing.

Abraham sowed the seed of his son, Isaac, on a mountain in the early morning. God not only provided a replacement sacrifice, He multiplied Abraham's wealth and descendants and gave him a giant piece of land. This unlocked a promised, willed estate to all of us.

God sowed the seed of His son, Jesus, on a hill on Good Friday and the seed rose from the ground on Easter. It multiplied into the salvation of the souls of all mankind. Then on Pentecost, His Spirit was poured out with the sound of a great wind; and the believers were filled with the Spirit.[7]

Do you feel the winds of change shifting? Is the economic breeze telling you that your vacation may need to be put on hold, that you

---

7   Acts 2

need to beef up your savings, or that your job may be in jeopardy? If so, fear not. Rather, it may be time to order a pizza and become a storm chaser. The Book of Psalms reminds us that:

> *"You stretch out the starry curtain of the heavens;*
> *you lay out the rafters of your home in the rain clouds.*
> *You make the clouds your chariot;*
> *you ride upon the wings of the wind.*
> *The winds are your messengers;*
> *flames of fire are your servants." (Psalm 104:2-4)*

This is the God of our economy. He uses shakings for us. He changes downturns into upturns. And when we are aligned with his vision, trusting that He will provide the seed and the wisdom we need for sowing, His is the economy of multiplication and blessing. He is the God of the wind and the rain. He is the God of the four seasons. He is the God of memory and hope. This is the same God who looks at the natural, the spiritual, and the economic storms and economic abundance and tells us the truth about His power in it.[8]

Release your tithe. Sow your seed. And live on your bread.

Live in peace with your money through God's economy and receive His abundance as you make room for His vision...and He makes room for you in that vision.

---

8 Mark 4:39